# Penny Stocks:

## Concise Edition

## Tony Pow

# Why you want to read this book

It should improve your financial health substantially.

- This book has about 85 pages (6*9) and is about double the size of its competitors with similar price range.

- A best seller was written by a young writer whose main income was from his books and none from his investing. Most of my income is from investing.

- Many popular books claiming the authors making millions. However, usually their techniques are hard to follow. Many admitted they had been bankrupted many times. My techniques minimize risking our money. Paper test your technique first.

- There are many popular books combining technical and some fundamentals. They worked very well at one time and folks making millions following the advices. However, look at their recent performances of the last five years.

- One book describes ROE as the only theme (with the story of the life of the author to fill up the book).

**My motivation to write this book**

I would like to share my experiences, both good and bad. I use simple-to-follow techniques using the free (or low-cost) resources available to us.

Click the link for the articles I wrote for SeekingAlpha.com, a site for investors. http://seekingalpha.com/author/tony-pow/articles

# Contents

## My micro cap performance

The strategies described here have been used in my book titled "Best Stocks 2014, According to Me". From 12/16/13 (the publish date) to 3/4/14, the list of all 135 selected stocks beat SPY by 103% and the list of 9 small cap stocks as you see below beat the SPY by almost 500%.

From 12/16/13 to 3/29/14 (today), the performances of the entire list of 9 small micro-cap stocks (RAS is not a micro-cap by my definition) are:

| Stock | Market Cap (M)[1] | Annualized Return |
|---|---|---|
| ARTX | 52 | 234% |
| CPSS | 176 | 6% |
| RAS | 602 | -19% |
| GST | 329 | 83% |
| EVC | 515 | 65% |
| LEE | 171 | 293% |
| SGU | 313 | 16% |
| HILL | 166 | 491% |
| MNTG | 147 | 12% |
| | | |
| Average | | 131% |
| SPY | | 22%[2] |
| Beat SPY by | | 496% |
| | | |

[1] As of 12/16/13
[2] Annualized return

## Disclaimer

Past performance does not guarantee future performance. I believe both the micro-cap and the market could have reached their temporary peaks by 4/2014. Please know that these stocks have not been tested in a down market.

# Introduction

They are risky as many of them do not have information as required by the SEC and the major exchanges. They are traded over the counter, OTC. They cannot be shorted (and most likely you do not want to do so even if it were allowed). Pier 1, Ford and many others were all penny stocks at one time.

Expect one winner for several losers; 1 winner for every 4 losers if I have to guess the ratio. However, the total profit could outpace the total loss if the strategy is properly implemented. The purpose of this book is to improve your odds of making a profit. Do not expect to be rich overnight.

You can buy 5000 shares at 1 cent each or one share of Apple in May 2013. When this penny stock moves up to 2 cents, you make 100%. This is not the reason to invest in penny stocks but it shows that they're very volatile. You may have a hard time trying to sell a penny stock as the average volume is very low.

Here are some good candidates.

- Established foreign companies such as Nestle and Sharp as of this writing. They want to avoid the expensive legal procedures and filing information periodically. Most are listed as pink sheets and they are not as risky as the other penny stocks.

- Fallen angels. They have been delisted due to low performance and /or the stock price falling below $1 (sometimes below $5). When they work around their problems, the stock prices may appreciate many times over. Most head to bankruptcy.

- Companies with new products such as a new technology or a new drug. They are moving up from development to the market phase of the product cycle. They may be acquired by larger companies. A recent example is the e-cigarette companies facing competition from the newly legalized drugs and/or the banning of e-cigarettes.

- New companies with quality products and/or technology. The business section of your local newspaper may have these candidates such as Aereo. Their products will most likely be challenged by the larger companies such as cable companies.

- Some could be hidden gems as no analysts have been following them. Talking about under value, I have seen one company with free cash more than its market cap!

- A money losing company could be a gem if it is developing a new technology or a new drug. Big companies such as Microsoft, Apple, and Google are consistently looking for this type of company to acquire.

Avoid the following stocks.

- Stocks that are set up as fraudulent companies. There are many small companies (foreign companies in particular) that are set up for this purpose. Even the well-established and well-funded companies fall into the trap from time to time. If they cannot spot these companies with all their resources, how can the retail investors spot them?

- Stocks with 25% or higher ownership by the owner and / or the family. Most never sell and never buy the stocks they own. There are exceptions and they are easily spotted by their fundamental metrics. For example, when a company's cash reserve is higher than its entire market cap and/or the P/Es is ridiculously low, evaluate it.

  Ensure the owners do not use it as their piggy bank for borrowing money, high compensation and/or granting options. When they do not have an independent board of directors, they can do whatever they want.

- Low volume stocks. It means you have to pay more to sell the stocks (i.e. the high spread between the ask price and the bid price).

  In addition, it is far easier to manipulate low-volume and/or low-priced stocks than large caps.

- "Pump-and-dump" strategy used by manipulators via mass email, radio/TV and news articles. The first ones may make money but the majority would lose their shirts. The 'tips' are the traps in disguise and the 'make believe' stories are bigger traps.

  As your mother would tell you, if it is too good to be true, most likely it is not.

If it is that good, why don't they act on it themselves and share this money-making idea with you, a stranger, at no charge? There is no free lunch!

- A company is running out of cash and/or heading to bankruptcy. A bargain price is no bargain.

You need to spend time to separate out the gems from garbage and fraudulent companies particularly in penny stocks. Some 'fundamentally sound' companies could be frauds as their financial statements can be manipulated.

Understand the company and its management. Call the company's investor relations department if they have one and they are willing to answer your phone call. Ask for their most updated financial statements and the prospectus of the company. Due to my limited time and a lot of stocks to evaluate, I have not done so myself.

**Finding and evaluating penny stocks**

Some penny stocks can only be discovered from friends or local newspapers. You should visit the company and/or talk to their investor relations person.

Besides the finance, ask how they use the capitalization and how the products/services stack up with the competition and their competitive edges. Investigate their managers' resumes and their history. Even ask how many years they have been in the current positions.

Check out whether the company files with the SEC from their website, a state regulator, or a business regulator such as a bank.

**Summary on how to reduce risk in penny stocks**

- Unless you have personal contact with the company which is not an established large foreign company, do not buy its stock.

- Even if they provide financial data, be careful as to whether they have been manipulated legally or illegally.

- Watch out for 'pump and dump'. These are quite common. Read the articles from the web carefully and ignore all your junk mails on promotions of any stock. If they are too good to be true, the writers will profit by buying the stock themselves. These days I see fewer junk mails of this kind than I had in the past.

- Avoid low-volume (with average daily volume less than 10,000 shares) and/or low-cap companies (with a market cap less than 50 million).

- Ensure the CEO is not using his company as an ATM.

- Some of the trading techniques are not applicable for penny stocks due to the low volume and high volatility. These are stop order (turning into market orders), market order, analyst coverage, selling short, day trading and options.

  Most of these companies do not make money initially and they do not pay dividends; they need to plow back the cash into their development / research. You need to consider whether the company has a niche in the market from its unique products and/or is following the market trend.

  The burn rate of the company and its ability to pay back loans are important. If the company burns 50% of its available cash, it can survive for two years just as an example. Most of these companies are under-capitalized.

  Many technical indicators may not work. The price and the volume of a stock can be easily manipulated to show a false uptrend.

**Links**
Scanning penny stocks:
https://www.youtube.com/watch?v=7iZpWmwBhel

**How this book is organized**

Most graphs are in landscape orientation for both paperback and e-readers. Some graphs may not be displayed adequately on a small screen of an e-reader. E-readers may be available in the current version of Windows, so you can read e-books on the larger screen of your PC. For better orientation, just flip the e-readers 90 degrees.

A link is usually included for these screens. Copy it to your browser to display the graphs on your PC if desirable. Instructions on how to produce some graphs are provided as you should try them out. One example is how to produce a chart on detecting market crashes.

It is easier to display some tables in landscape mode, which can be selected in your e-reader. Select a table or a graph via your e-reader to display it to fit the screen.

The font size and page size of most e-book formats can be adjusted. The unknown, special character is the "smiling face" that the current Kindle does not convert correctly as of this writing.

There are clickable links to web articles. Most of them are from my own websites and public websites such as Wikipedia. Some public links may not be available in the future as they are not under my control.

Fidelity Video provides video clips to explain some basic terms and it may require Fidelity customers to sign on in order to view them. Check the trial offer from Fidelity. YouTube offers similar video lessons.

These links extend the usefulness of this book by making available specific topics that may not be interesting to every reader.

The current version provides most of the links the paperback readers can enter into your browser. Get the same information by entering a search in Wikipedia such as Dogs of Dow.

Investopedia is another source beside Wikipedia.
http://www.investopedia.com/

'Afterthoughts' includes my additional comments and comments from others. Readers can make comments in this book's website. These comments may be included in the Afterthoughts in subsequent revisions, with the commenter's last name redacted. It is the section of the article for freer and informal discussion.

For convenience, this book uses SPY, an Exchange Traded Fund (ETF) simulating the S&P 500, as the benchmark for the market.

Annualized returns (Return * 365 / (Days between)) are used where appropriate for more meaningful comparison. To illustrate, I have a 10% return in 6 months, a 10% in a year and a 10% in 2 years. It is more meaningful to use annualized returns of 20%, 10% and 5% respectively for the 6-month return, the one-year return and the 2-year return in this example.

Usually I do not include the dividend, so you can add an estimated 1.5% to the annualized return. In addition, compound interest is not used for easier calculation, so the actual return could be even better.

## About the author

I graduated from Cal. State University at San Jose in Industrial Engineering and University of Mass. in Amherst with a MS in Industrial Engineering. My last job was in IT. I have been an investor for over 30 years. My articles in SeekingAlpha.com.

## Dedication

To all retail investors and future retail investors including my grandchildren. I sincerely hope this book will build bridges with fellow investors with different backgrounds.

**Acknowledgement** Thanks to Seeking Alpha, Fidelity, Wikipedia and Investopedia for the many helpful links to enrich this book. Thanks to Yahoo!Finance and Finviz.com for the tools and charts used in this book.

## Important notices

| Version | Paperback | e-Book |
|---------|-----------|---------|
| 1.0 | 05/2014 | 05/2014 |
| 2.3 | 08/2017 | 08/2017 |
| 3.0 | 10/2019 | 10/2019 |
| 3.3 | 10/2021 | 10/2021 |

Book store managers can order the printed books from Createspace.com.
https://tonyp4idea.blogspot.com/2020/12/book-managers.html

Book update.
https://ebmyth.blogspot.com/2020/12/updates-for-all-books.html

Disclaimer

Do not gamble with money that you cannot afford to lose. Past performance is a guideline and is not necessarily indicative of future results. All information is believed to be accurate, but there it is not a guarantee. All the strategies including charts to detect market plunges described have no guarantee that they will make money and they may lose money. Do not trade without doing due diligence and be warned that most data may be obsolete. All my articles and the associated data are for informational and illustration purposes only. I'm not a professional investment counselor or a tax professional. Seek one before you make any investment decisions. The above mentioned also applies for all other advice such as on accounting, taxes, health and any topic mentioned in this book. I am not a professional in any of these fields. Most of the time, I use annualized for a better comparison; 5% in a month is more than 4% in a year for example. For simplicity, most of my returns do not include commissions, exchange fees, order spread and dividends. Same for all the links contained in this book. Some articles may offend some one or some organization unintentionally. If I did, I'm sorry about that. I am politically and religiously neutral. I provide my best efforts to ensure the accuracy of my articles. Data also from different sources was believed to be accurate. However, there is no guarantee that they are accurate and suitable for the current market conditions and /or your individual situations. The values of some parameters such as RSI(14) are arbitrarily set by me. My publisher and I are not liable for any damages in using this book or its contents.

# 1	Penny stocks

They are risky as many of them do not have information as required by the SEC and the major exchanges. They are traded over the counter, OTC. They cannot be shorted (and most likely you do not want to do so even if it were allowed). Pier 1, Ford and many others were all penny stocks at one time.

Expect one winner for several losers; 1 winner for every 4 losers if I have to guess the ratio. However, the total profit could outpace the total loss if the strategy is properly implemented. The purpose of this book is to improve your odds of making a profit. Do not expect to be rich overnight.

You can buy 5000 shares at 1 cent each or one share of Apple in May 2013. When this penny stock moves up to 2 cents, you make 100%. This is not the reason to invest in penny stocks but it shows that they're very volatile. You may have a hard time trying to sell a penny stock as the average volume is very low.

Here are some good candidates.

- Established foreign companies such as Nestle and Sharp as of this writing. They want to avoid the expensive legal procedures and filing information periodically. Most are listed as pink sheets and they are not as risky as the other penny stocks.

- Fallen angels. They have been delisted due to low performance and /or the stock price falling below $1 (sometimes below $5). When they work around their problems, the stock prices may appreciate many times over. Most head to bankruptcy.

- Companies with new products such as a new technology or a new drug. They are moving up from development to the market phase of the product cycle. They may be acquired by larger companies. A recent example is the e-cigarette companies facing competition from the newly legalized drugs and/or the banning of e-cigarettes.

- New companies with quality products and/or technology. The business section of your local newspaper may have these candidates such as Aereo. Their products will most likely be challenged by the larger companies such as cable companies.

- Some could be hidden gems as no analysts have been following them. Talking about under value, I have seen one company with free cash more than its market cap!

- A money losing company could be a gem if it is developing a new technology or a new drug. Big companies such as Microsoft, Apple, and Google are consistently looking for this type of company to acquire.

Avoid the following stocks.

- Stocks that are set up as fraudulent companies. There are many small companies (foreign companies in particular) that are set up for this purpose. Even the well-established and well-funded companies fall into the trap from time to time. If they cannot spot these companies with all their resources, how can the retail investors spot them?

- Stocks with 25% or higher ownership by the owner and / or the family. Most never sell and never buy the stocks they own. There are exceptions and they are easily spotted by their fundamental metrics. For example, when a company's cash reserve is higher than its entire market cap and/or the P/Es is ridiculously low, evaluate it.

  Ensure the owners do not use it as their piggy bank for borrowing money, high compensation and/or granting options. When they do not have an independent board of directors, they can do whatever they want.

- Low volume stocks. It means you have to pay more to sell the stocks (i.e. the high spread between the ask price and the bid price).

  In addition, it is far easier to manipulate low-volume and/or low-priced stocks than large caps.

- "Pump-and-dump" strategy used by manipulators via mass email, radio/TV and news articles. The first ones may make money but the majority would lose their shirts. The 'tips' are the traps in disguise and the 'make believe' stories are bigger traps.

  As your mother would tell you, if it is too good to be true, most likely it is not.

If it is that good, why don't they act on it themselves and share this money-making idea with you, a stranger, at no charge? There is no free lunch!

- A company is running out of cash and/or heading to bankruptcy. A bargain price is no bargain.

You need to spend time to separate out the gems from garbage and fraudulent companies particularly in penny stocks. Some 'fundamentally sound' companies could be frauds as their financial statements can be manipulated.

Understand the company and its management. Call the company's investor relations department if they have one and they are willing to answer your phone call. Ask for their most updated financial statements and the prospectus of the company. Due to my limited time and a lot of stocks to evaluate, I have not done so myself.

**Finding and evaluating penny stocks**

Some penny stocks can only be discovered from friends or local newspapers. You should visit the company and/or talk to their investor relations person.

Besides the finance, ask how they use the capitalization and how the products/services stack up with the competition and their competitive edges. Investigate their managers' resumes and their history. Even ask how many years they have been in the current positions.

Check out whether the company files with the SEC from their website, a state regulator, or a business regulator such as a bank.

**Summary on how to reduce risk in penny stocks**

- Unless you have personal contact with the company which is not an established large foreign company, do not buy its stock.

- Even if they provide financial data, be careful as to whether they have been manipulated legally or illegally.

- Watch out for 'pump and dump'. These are quite common. Read the articles from the web carefully and ignore all your junk mails on promotions of any stock. If they are too good to be true, the writers will profit by buying the stock themselves. These days I see fewer junk mails of this kind than I had in the past.

- Avoid low-volume (with average daily volume less than 10,000 shares) and/or low-cap companies (with a market cap less than 50 million).

- Ensure the CEO is not using his company as an ATM.

- Some of the trading techniques are not applicable for penny stocks due to the low volume and high volatility. These are stop order (turning into market orders), market order, analyst coverage, selling short, day trading and options.

  Most of these companies do not make money initially and they do not pay dividends; they need to plow back the cash into their development / research. You need to consider whether the company has a niche in the market from its unique products and/or is following the market trend.

  The burn rate of the company and its ability to pay back loans are important. If the company burns 50% of its available cash, it can survive for two years just as an example. Most of these companies are under-capitalized.

  Many technical indicators may not work. The price and the volume of a stock can be easily manipulated to show a false uptrend.

**Links**
Scanning penny stocks:
https://www.youtube.com/watch?v=7iZpWmwBhel

# Filler: The ideal program

I'm writing a program named IYBID (in your best interest, dummy) making all government decisions and to include twitting. It will be born and made in the USA.

## 2 Micro caps

I enjoy micro caps (stocks between 50M to 300M according to the SEC) more than penny stocks as they're less risky. When they're listed in one of the three major exchanges, we have a lot of info from the required filings of these companies. The tools to track other stocks can be applied to these stocks too. However, you may have a hard time finding articles on these stocks.

When these stocks move up to mid cap and even large cap, it could mean huge appreciation. Eventually and hopefully they will be included in one of the indexes, and this would boost up the stock prices automatically, as some ETFs are required to buy them.

#Filler: Tips

When you trade 5 times or more a week, investigate whether you're eligible to trade as a business by the current tax rule. A business allows its owner to deduct business expenses.

If you create a trading plan on when and how to trade and then monitor your trades periodically, you would likely become more disciplined and a better investor.

Monitor your trades. You may need to take a breather or switch to paper trading if you have a few losses in a row. Paper trading would be useful and it serves as part of the education.

You should keep a trading log or journal to review what you may or have done wrong, and then learn from that. This may be part of the tuition for trading and there are always lessons to learn. This book can help you to reduce errors but there is no substitution for actual experiences with real money.

Technical analysis (a.k.a. charts) may not be good for penny stocks as their trade volumes are usually low. However, using charts for market timing is fine.

Be careful when using a historical database to test screens / strategies. Penny stocks have more of a chance for survivorship bias. If you have two stocks, one down to zero and one up by 100%, your total return of these 2 stocks should be zero. It could be 100% up if the database took out the losing stock. It means you never find this losing stock in your test as it is not in your database.

## 3  Summary

Microcap stocks have more regulations and usually higher volume than penny stocks. I prefer microcap stocks.

**Profit and risk**

Penny stocks have the highest profit potential, but they are also the riskiest compared to microcap stocks. It depends on your own risk tolerance when selecting which category you want to trade.

I recommend to paper trade and gradually move up to a larger percent of your portfolio. Expect your money to be tied up for a long time due to the low volatility in both volume and price. Be emotionally detached.

Do not put more than 5% of your portfolio on one stock. Unless you understand the company thoroughly and the fundamentals are very sound, making a fast 50% profit in a micro-cap stock is better than making 200% in penny stocks that have a chance of losing all value.

There are many different definitions of penny stocks. To me, usually they are stocks less than $5 and they are trades under the OTC-BB and/or named pink sheets. Exceptions abound. Refer to Wikipedia and Investopedia for their general definitions.

**How to start**

Open an account with your broker. Some have restrictions and/or higher commissions for penny stocks. Some provide paper trading so it is good for beginners to try this without risking their money. Paper trading for penny stocks sometimes are misleading due to the low volumes. Most provide limited or no research to penny stocks and micro caps.

**When to buy**

When the market is plunging, do not buy any stock (actually you should sell most of your stock holdings especially small caps). Some small caps may not recover. Buy them back when the market is recovering as most will increase their values at a faster rate.

**What to buy**

Do not depend your buy decisions on tips, emails and mail. Most are 'pump-and-dump' type of schemes. Do not listen to your brokers who have very high commissions and incentives to sell you penny stocks as illustrated in the movie Wolf of Wall Street.

Also avoid bankrupting companies (usually they have a Q at the end of their symbol). They are still listed for now. When some emerge from bankruptcy, most likely they will issue new shares and the old ones usually have 0 value.

However, if the blueprint of the company is workable for recovery and/or the company has enough assets including patented technology, customer base, and valuable inventory for example, they may have a chance to turn around in the future.

IPOs of small companies that have great products / services are promising candidates. Spend time in evaluating the products, the company's business plan, qualifications of employees and the track record of the management team. They are risky but it could bring huge profits. 2015 was not a good profit year in buying IPO stocks, but the previous two years were.

Most penny stocks have limited information from the web such as from Seeking Alpha. You may want to check out the company's website that would include financial statements, product descriptions and hopefully their business model.

Financial statements indicate how the company did in the last quarter and last year. Check out the date of the statement.

There are often few write-ups on penny stocks and most microcap stocks. Furthermore, you should not depend on the financial statements of penny stocks. You must know the company inside out. Call the company's investor relationship department or visit the local company if it is close to you.

Check out any warnings from the SEC from its website.

Here are some positive developments. The official of a small company explained that during a recession, the company did not expand their marketing effort, but expanded in the research department.

Besides the profit and its valuation (P/E), the products are the most important. Are they competitive in the current market? Even so, it cannot tell you whether they're competitive in the near future.

Check out their business models. Some do not make sense such as most internet companies were during its bubble era in 2000.

Intangible events that are not usually included in the financial statements are: potential lawsuits, expiration or the trial results of a drug, quitting of a major employee and losing a key customer.

Avoid developing countries especially with their small companies. Even if their financial statements look good, they may be frauds as I have learned the same lesson the hard way many times.

Diversifying is more important with penny and microcap stocks. Allocate no more than 5% (less in a falling market) of your portfolio on these stocks. I prefer to hold 10 penny and microcap stocks instead of one. For taxable accounts, sell losers within a year to offset any short-term gains.

Use Stock Level 2 Quotes to show you how many buy orders and sell orders are lined up. Avoid stocks with few buy orders. In many cases, there is a market maker controlling the tempo and direction of a particular stock. Charts (Candlestick recommended) also show the price and volume. It requires you to spend more time on looking at the evolving charts.
http://www.investopedia.com/articles/trading/06/level2quotes.asp

**What and when to sell**

You may want to set up a target price and a price to protect from further losses. Limit Loss orders available from most brokers does not guarantee the execution of the order. Stop Loss guarantees the execution, but the market order may be at the low price of the spread. Stop loss orders may not work as the spread is too wide for low volume stocks.

Some stocks skyrocket, and some even move up to major exchanges. Patience could pay off big time. I prefer to sell at a 25% loss and adjust the loss according to the current price (not the initial price you paid for). There is no bullet-proof strategy.

**Conclusion**

Penny stocks are the riskiest but the most profitable stocks. Personally I prefer micro caps that are more regulated. Monitor your strategy and adjust it accordingly. If you're doing far better in penny stocks than micro caps, stick with penny stocks, and vice versa.

## Section I: Simple techniques

For starters, just trade ETFs such as SPY (an ETF simulating the market), and you can skip the rest of the book. It only take a few minutes every month to time the market. When the market is not plunging, buy or keep SPY (or any ETF that stimulates the market); otherwise sell it. Do the opposite when the market is recovering. The simple technique described later does not find the peak and bottom of the market, but hopefully saves you further loss during a market crash and advises you return to the market. There will be some false alarms, but they will tell you returning to the market briefly. Hence, the damage is minimal.

If you have less than $50,000 to invest, just buy ETFs. Improve your investing skills by reading investment articles from this book and your broker's website. For example, Fidelity has a lot of information for investors.

Subscription to AAII is recommended. When your portfolio grows more than $50,000, invest on a subscription such as Value Line, Zacks or IBD (more for momentum traders). Initially, use the information for paper trading on value stocks, which is usually available from brokers. With the recent GameStop incident, do NOT think buying a hedge fund is a good bet.

For the long term, knowledge is most important in your investing life and experience comes next. Retail investors have a lot of advantages over fund managers. However, I advise you NOT to be a trader. Hence, you should ignore the 'fabulous' trade systems that claim to be very profitable. Statistically most amateur traders lose money as they cannot compete with experienced, disciplined traders.

### How to start

I recommend trading ETFs first and when the market is not risky. The very basic terms such as ETF are not fully explained here; try Investopedia for terms you need to know. Otherwise this book would be doubled in size and it would bore most readers. Investopedia, your broker's website (especially Fidelity) and AAII (requiring subscription) provide many excellent articles. Alternatively, buy a book for beginners. Here are some freebies:

Click here for Morningstar classroom.
http://morningstar.com/cover/classroom.html
Click here for Vanguard.
https://investor.vanguard.com/investing/investor-education
Click here for Investopedia's Tutorials.

http://www.investopedia.com/university/
Click here for Yahoo!
http://finance.yahoo.com/education/begin_investing
Click here for Fidelity basic in investing.
https://www.fidelity.com/investment-guidance/investing-basics

# 1    Simplest market timing

### Why market timing

Before 2000, market timing was a waste of time. However after that, we have had two market plunges with the average loss of about 45%. It sounds harder to time the market than it actually is. We have a simple technique to detect market plunges and when to reenter the market. Our objective is reducing the loss to 25%.

Market timing depends on charts; the following describes how to use chart information without creating charts. Most charts will not identify the peaks and bottoms of the market as they depend on data (i.e. the stock prices). However, it would reduce further loses. It is simpler than it sounds. Just follow the procedure below.

The first part of this technique detects market plunges, and the second part advises you when to reenter the market. It applies to individual stocks too. It also works to detect the trend of a sector (entering an ETF for the specific sector instead of SPY) and a specific stock.

How to detect market plunges without charts (a.k.a. **Death Cross**)
1.  Bring up Finviz.com.
2.  Enter SPY (or any ETF that simulates the market) or RSP for equally weighed SPY.
3.  If SMA-200% is positive, it indicates that the market plunge has not been detected and you can skip the following steps.
4.  The market is plunging if SMA-50% is more negative than SMA-200%. To illustrate this condition, SMA-200% is -2% and SMA-50% is -5%.
5.  Sell most stocks starting with the riskiest ones first such as the ones with negative earnings, high P/Es and/or high Debt/Equity. Obtain this info from Finviz.com by entering the symbol of the stock you own.
6.  Conservative investors should sell only those overpriced stocks. Aggressive investors should sell all stocks. Extremely aggressive investors should sell all stocks, buy contra ETFs, and even short stocks. I do not recommend beginners to be aggressive.

7.  Alternately, you can use SMA-20 and SMA-50 for quicker detection at the expense of more false alarm.

## When to return to the market (a.k.a. Golden Cross)

Use the above in a reversed sense to detect whether the market has been recovering. However, when the SMA-200% turns positive, I would start buying value stocks (low P/E but the 'E' has to be positive, and/or low Debt/Equity).

1.  Bring up Finviz.com.
2.  Enter SPY (or any ETF that simulates the market).
3.  If SMA-200% is negative, the market is not recovering, and you can skip the following steps.
4.  Sell all contra ETFs and close all shorts if you have any.
5.  Market recovery is confirmed when SMA-50% is more positive than SMA-200%. To illustrate this condition, SMA-200% is 2% and SMA-50% is 5%. Commit a large percent of cash (or all cash for aggressive investors) to stocks. If you do not know what to buy, buy SPY or an ETF that simulates the market.

## How often to check the market timing indicators

Do the above once a month. When the SPY price is closer to SMA actions percentage, perform the above once a week. The charts and data for market timing described in this book are based on SMA-350 (Simple Moving Average) that is more preferable than this simple procedure, but it requires some simple charting.

## Nothing is perfect

If the market timing is perfect, there would be no poor folks. The major 'defects' are:
*   It does not detect the peak / bottom as it depends on past data. However, it would save you a lot during the crash.
*   It is hard to determine whether it is a correction or a crash.
*   From 2000 to 2010, there is only one false signal. The indicator tells you to exit and then tell you reenter the market shortly. In most cases, you do not lose a lot. After 2010, we have more false signals.
*   The market may not be rational or may be influenced due to specific conditions such as excessive printing of USD.
*   If you do not mind charting, use SMA 350 (or 400) using SPY. Buy when the price is above SMA-350 (or SMA-400), and sell otherwise. SMA-400 reduces the number of false signals but not nimble.

Link: 4 signals of overvalued market:
https://www.youtube.com/watch?v=f5pyy3xoadE

# 2     Quick analysis of ETFs

**Evaluate an ETF**

ETFs are a basket of stocks according to the market, a specific sector, country or a specific theme.

Yahoo!Finance used to give the P/E of an ETF. Try to get it from ETFdb.com. Enter the symbol of the ETF such as XLU, and then select Valuation. If it is below 15 and above zero, it could be a value ETF. Also, if the current price is lower than its NAV, it is sold at a discount (or premium vice versa). Compare its YTD Return to SPY's.

Alternatively, get similar info from http://www.multpl.com/. In addition, this website provides the following metrics: Shiller P/E, Price/Sales, and Price/Book.

From Finviz.com, enter the ETF symbol. If SMA-20%, SMA-50% and SMA-200% are all positive, most likely the ETF is in an uptrend. To illustrate, SMA-200 is Simple Moving Average for the last 200 trading sessions (no trading on weekends and specific holidays). The percent is how much the stock price of the ETF is above the SMA. If the percent is negative, it means the stock price is below the SMA.

If your average holding period of your stocks is about 50 days, SMA-50% is more appropriate to you.

If RSI(14) > 65, it is probably oversold; if it is < 30, it is probably under-sold (indicating value).

In addition, ensure the ETF's average volume is high (I suggest more than 10,000 shares), the market cap is more than 300 M, and it has low fees. Most popular ETFs have these characteristics. Beginners should avoid leveraged ETFs.

**How to determine if the sector has been recovered**
It is easier to profit by following the uptrend of an ETF using the above info. It is hard to detect when the bottom of an ETF has been reached. If SMA-20%, SMA-50% and SMA-200% are all positive, most likely the ETF is in an uptrend or it has recovered. It does not always happen as predicted, so use stops to protect your investment

**Chief factors to select an ETF**

Statistically, the market is in an uptrend most of the time. However, the last two market crashes, the market loses an average of about 45%. If the market is crashing, the contra ETFs (betting against the market or sector) have higher chance of profit.

Most investors trade passive ETFs (as opposed to active ETFs) based on the market or a specific category of the market such as commodity and market cap. If you are more aggressive (not recommended for beginners), select leveraged ETFs. Besides the SMAs described, there are several factors to select an ETF (all should available in free sites such as ETFdb.com:

- Market size. A larger size should minimize the fees, usually provides better research and maintaining, and better volatility.
- Fee. Some ETFs based on the same index could have different fees. Check out their performances, and select the one with the lower fee.
- Years in period. A new ETF may not have enough data for evaluation. However, a new ETF usually addresses a new sector or sub sector and it could be profitable.
- Family. A reputable ETF family is more reliable to me. The ETFs within the family can share research and operations efficiently. The big three are iShares (with major ETF IVV), Vanguard (VTI) and SPDR (SPY).
- Performance esp. import for active ETFs. Check the average performance for the last 3 years or possibly during bear market.

**An example**

First, determine whether the market is risky. Most beginners should not invest in a risky market. Advanced investors can bet against the market or a specific sector by buying contra ETFs or puts.

Next, you want to limit the number of sector ETFs by selecting those that are either in an uptrend or hitting bottom (bottom is hard to predict). Personally I prefer sectors with long-term uptrends (indicated by articles found in many websites including cnnfn.com and Seeking Alpha.

For illustration purposes only for deteriorating market conditions, I would select the following ETFs: SPY (simulating the market based on large companies) and XLP (consumer staples). XLP should perform better than XLY (consumer discretionary) during a recession as those products are the necessities.

Technical indicators such as SMA-50 (Simple Moving Average for the last 50 sessions), SMA-200 and RSI(14) are obtained from Finviz.com and the rest are obtained from Yahoo!Finance.com. After you buy the ETF, use a stop loss to protect your investment. For example, bio tech sector moved up for many months until it crashed in 2015. Change the stop loss value every month to protect your gains in this case.

| As of 2/5/2016 | SPY | XLP (staples) | XLY (discret.) |
|---|---|---|---|
| Price | 190 | 50 | 71 |
| NAV | 192 | 50 | 73 |
| • Technical | | | |
| SMA-50 | -4% | 0% | -7% |
| SMA-200 | -6% | 2% | -7% |
| RSI(14) | 44 | 50 | 36 |
| Other | Double bottom at $186 | | |
| • Fundamental | | | |
| P/E | 17 | 20 | 19 |
| Yield | 2.1% | 2.5% | 1.5% |
| YTD return | -5% | 0.5% | -5% |
| Net asset | 174 B | 9 B | 10 B |
| | | | |

Explanation
- The figures may not be identical among websites due to the dates they are using.
- XLY has best discount among the 3 ETFs as most investors believe a recession is coming.
- XLP has less down trend among the 3 ETFs as expected.
- XLY is more undersold among the three as expected.
- Double bottom is a technical pattern that indicates the stock would surge upward.
- SPY has a better value according to its P/E.
- XLY's dividend is the least among the three as they have more tech companies in the ETF. They have to plow back the profits to research and development.
- XLP has the best YTD return among the three.
- As long as the asset is above 500 M (200 M for specialized ETFs), it is fine and all three pass this mark.

There are many metrics such as Debt/Equity not readily available from most websites. Many sites list the top holdings of a specific ETF. Just average the metrics of the top ten or so of its stock holdings.

## Check out the major stocks in an ETF

This example evaluates RING, a gold miner, using ETFdb and Finviz that are free from the web. The data is from July, 6, 2020.

Bring up ETFdb and enter RING in the search. There are basic info that are important to me: Sector (gold miners), Asset Size (Large-Cap), Issuer (iShares), Inception (Jan. 31, 2012), Expense Ratio (0.39%) and Tax Form (1099).

They fit all my requirements. The expense ratio is higher than most ETFs that simulating an index such as SPY. I try to trade ETFs using Tax Form 1099 in my taxable accounts. The large cap created about 8 years ago by a reputable company are good.

Select "Dividend and Valuation". P/E of 17.39 is fine in a rank of 11 in 27 in similar group of ETFs. As in my books, I stated it is hard to evaluate miners. I buy this ETF primarily to fight the possibility of inflation and the potential depreciation of USD. The dividend rate of 0.52% (0.70% from Finviz) is in the low range of the scale; it is fine for me as dividend is not my concern.

There are more info from this website. For simplicity, bring up Finviz:
- The short-term trend is up (SMA-20% = 8% and SMA-50% = 7%).
- The long-term trend is up (SMA-200% = 26%).
- It is close to overbought (RSI(14) = 64%; 65% to me is overbought).
- It is -4% from 52-w High. It has performed well from the YTD, Last Year, Last Quarter, Last Month and Last Week.
- It almost doubles in price from mid March this year.
- Avg. Vol. is fine.

From ETFdb, check the Holding. It has 39 stocks, so it is quite diversified for this industry. The two top holdings are NEM (19%) and ABX (18%), which is listed as GOLD in NYSX. I also consider to buy these two stocks in addition to RING. You can estimate the other metrics that are not available by averaging these two stocks. Here is my summary:

| STOCK | NEM | GOLD |
|---|---|---|
| Forward P/E | 20 | 25 |
| Debt / Share | 0.31 | 0.24 |
| ROE | 17% | 22% |
| Sales Q/Q | 43% | 30% |
| EPS Q/Q | 389% | 254% |
| SMA50 | 2% | 4% |
| RSI(14) | 59% | 60% |
| Insider Trans | -13% | N/A |
| Fidelity's Equity Summary Score | 6.1 | 6.8 |

# 3      Rotate four ETFs

We can beat the market by rotating one ETF that represents the market such as SPY and cash via market timing. Aggressive investors can add SH or PSQ (contra ETFs) to the four to have better returns during market plunges.

During a market uptrend, rotating the following four ETFs could be more profitable than staying with SPY (or any ETF that simulating the market). Be warned that a short-term capital gain in taxable accounts is not treated as favorably as the long-term capital gain; check current tax laws.

The allocation percentages depend on your individual risk tolerance. You can use indexed mutual funds. Compare their expenses and restrictions. Some mutual funds charge you if you withdraw within a specific time period.

Select the best performer of last month (from Seeking Alpha, cnnFn, or one of many ETF/mutual fund sites). Add a contra ETF such as SH to take advantage of a falling market for more aggressive investors.  Add sector ETFs to the described four ETFs such as XLY, XLP, XLE, XLF, XLU, IYW, XHB, IYM, OIL and XLU to expand your selection.

| ETFs | Money Market | U.S. | International | Bond |
|---|---|---|---|---|
| Fidelity | | Spartan Total Market | Spartan Global Market | Spartan US Bond |
| Vanguard | | Total Stock Market | Total International Market | Total Bond Market |
| My choice | Fidelity | SPY | Vanguard | Fidelity |
| | | | | |
| Suggest % | | | | |
| During Market plunge | 90% | 0% | 0% | 10% |
| After plunge | 10% | 60% | 20% | 10% |

## Explanation
- The above are suggestions only. If your broker offers similar ETFs, consider using them.
- Check out any restrictions of the ETFs and commissions.

- 4 ETFs (one actually is a money market fund) are enough for most starters. They are diversified, low-cost and you do not need rebalancing except during a market plunge.
- The percentages are suggestions only. If you are less risk tolerant, allocate more to a money market fund, CD and/or bond ETF.
- Have at least 10% allocated to the money market fund for safety.
- When the market is risky, reduce stock equities (i.e. increase money market and bond allocations).
- The symbols for Fidelity ETFs are FSTMX, FSGDX and FBIDX.
- The symbols for Vanguard ETFs are VTSMX, VGTSX and VBMFX.
- If you are more advanced, use additional sector ETFs to rotate. Also buy long-term bond funds (such as 30-year Treasury) when the interest rates is 10% or more.

# 4    Simplest way to evaluate stocks

Beginners should trade ETFs only. This chapter is for the readers who are ready or getting ready to trade stocks. In general, ETFs are diversified, less volatile than trading stocks. However, stocks offer higher profit but higher risk.

Many stock researches have already been done recently and some are available free of charge. I have no affiliation with Fidelity except I retired from it. You can open an account with them with no balance. Their Equity Summary Score is one of the best indicators; I check out **value** stocks with score higher than 8. Concentrate on fundamental metrics such as P/E for long-term holds, and momentum metrics for short-term holds. Add criteria to limit the number of screened stocks. Finviz.com is a free screener.

**Several sources**
The popular ones are Morningstar, Value Line, The Street and Zacks (currently free for rankings of individual stocks). If they are not free, check out whether they are available from your local library. I have 3 simple ways to evaluate stocks starting with the simplest. In addition, read the articles on the selected stocks from Fidelity, Finviz, Seeking Alpha and many other sources for further evaluation.

**Fidelity**

Select only stocks that have Fidelity's Equity Summary Score 8 or higher. There are tons of information about a stock. Once a while I did not agree with the score such as SHOP and ZM that scored high in August, 2020. Include the following for your analysis.

**A modified stock selection based on a magazine article**

Most metrics are available from Finviz except EV/EBITDA.

1. Forward P/E (expected earnings and not based on the last twelve months). It should range from 5 to 15 (10 to 25 for high tech stocks). EV/EBITDA (from Yahoo!Finance) is a better choice as it includes the debts and cash than P/E; it would be more effective if it uses forward earnings. If you do not use EV/EBITDA, ensure Debt/Equity is less than 0.5 except for the debt-intensive industries.

2. ROE (Return of Equity) measures how well the company uses the capital. I prefer stocks with ROE greater than 5%.

3. Volatility. Conservative investors should select stocks with a beta of less than one (i.e. less volatile).

4. Insider Transactions for sales (i.e. negative) from should be less than 5%. If it is -5%, most likely the insiders are dumping it.

5. Compare the metrics such as P/E and Debt/Equity to its five-year average and its competitors (available in Fidelity).

6. Momentum. Check out the SMA-50 (actually SMA-50%) and SMA-200. Ideally they should be positive. SMA-50% is especially important for stocks you do not want to keep for a long time.

7. Check out articles on the stock as some recent events (for example a new lawsuit) have not been included in the metrics.

8. Compare the trend of the sector this stock is in. Under Finviz, enter the related sector ETF.

**Summary**
The sources are Fidelity (Equity Summary Score and various comparisons), Finviz and Yahoo!Finance (for EV/EBITDA). Value stocks should be held longer.

| Category | Score / Metric | Value /Momentum |
|---|---|---|
| **Score** | Fidelity's Equity Summary Score | Both |
| | | |
| **Value** | EV/EBITDA | Value |
| | P/E cheaper compared to 5-year avg. | Value |
| | P/E cheaper compared to its sector. | Value |
| | Insider Purchases | Both |
| | | |
| **Safety** | Debt/Equity | Value |
| | Compare it to its sector. | Value |
| | | |
| **Momentum** | 50-SMA% | Momentum |
| | 200-SMA% (for long term holds). | Value |
| | | |
| **Articles** | Check out latest events | Both |
| | | |
| **Market** | No purchase if market is risky. | Momentum |

## A simple scoring system using Finviz

Bring up Finviz.com and then enter the stock symbol.

| No. | Metric | Good | Bad | Score |
|---|---|---|---|---|
| 1 | Forward P/E[1] | Between 2.5 and 12.5,   Score  = 2 | > 50 or < 0, Score = -1 | |
| 2 | P/ FCF[1] | < 12,   Score  = 1 | >30 or < 0, Score = -1 | |
| 3 | P/S[1] | < 0.8, Score  = 1 | < 0, Score = -1 | |
| 4 | P/ B[1] | < 1,   Score  = 1 | < 0, Score = -1 | |
| | Compare quarter to quarter of last year | | | |
| 5 | Sales Q/Q | > 15%,   Score = 1 | < 0, Score = -1 | |
| 6 | EPS Q/Q | > 20% ,  Score = 1 | < 0, Score = -1 | |
| | | | | |
| | | | **Grand Score** | |
| | Stock Symbol  Date[2] | Current Price | SPY | |

Footnote

[1]    Negative values for Sales (due to accounting adjustments), Equity and Book are possible but not likely.

[2]    The last row is for your information only. SPY is used to measure whether it will beat the market by comparing the return of this stock to the return of SPY.

## The Score

Score each metric and sum up all the scores giving the Grand Score. If the Grand Score is 3, the stock passes this scoring system. Even if it is a 2, it still deserves further analysis if you have time. You may want to add scores from other vendors. To illustrate on using Fidelity, add 1 to the score if Fidelity's Equity Summary score is 8 or higher. Monitor the performance after every 6 months or so to see whether this scoring system beats the market.

## Very basic advice for beginners

Beginners should stick with U.S. stocks with Market Cap greater than 800 M (million), Debt/Equity less than .25 (25%) except for debt-intensive industries such as utilities and airlines and Forward P/E between 5 to 20 (25 for high-tech companies). These metrics are all available from Finviz.com, which is free.

Do not have more than 20% of your portfolio in one stock (unless it is an ETF or mutual fund) and do not have more than 30% of your portfolio in one sector.

For more conservative investors, buy non-volatile stocks whose beta (available from Yahoo!Finance) is less than 1. Beta of 1 represents the market (the S&P 500 index). For example, a stock with beta 1.5 statistically fluctuates more than 50% of the market and hence it is very volatile.

Try paper trading to check out your strategy and your skill in trading stocks. If your broker does not provide one, use a spreadsheet to record your trades or check the availability of simulator.investopedia.com.

#Filler: Silence is golden

I am glad I did not give advice to a friend who had to decide whether to take a lump sum payment or an annuity. The correction in March, 2020 would wipe out a lot of his portfolio if he took the lump sum payment. No one would share his profits when the predictions are correct, but the blame if it does not materialize.

It is same in investing that nothing is certain. With educated guesses, we should have more rights than wrongs especially in the long run.

## 5    Simplest technical analysis

When the stock, the sector that the stock is in and the market are all above its SMA-N averages (Single Moving Average for the last N sessions), most likely the stock is trending up.

1. Bring up Finviz.com from your browser.
2. Enter SPY. Write down the SMA-200 (Single Moving Average for 200 sessions). Positive numbers indicate that the trend for the market is up.

   However, the market could be peaking or overbought. Be careful when SMA-200 is over 5% and / or RSI(14) is over 65%. RSI is a metric on over bought / under bought.
3. Enter the sector ETF the stock is in. Write down the SMA-50. Positive numbers indicate that trend for the sector is up.

   However, the sector could be peaking or overbought. Be careful when the SMA-200 is over 10% and / or RSI(14) is over 65%.
4. Enter the stock symbol. If your average holding period of the stocks is 200, use SMA-200 and so on. I recommend SMA-200 for holding value stocks long term and SMA-50 for momentum stocks. Write down the SMA-N for your stock. Positive numbers indicate that the trend is up.

   However, the stock could be peaking or overbought. Be careful when the SMA-200 (or SMA-50) is over 25% and / or RSI(14) is over 65%.

If the above three criteria and the fundamental criteria are satisfied, most likely it is a good buy. If you buy sector ETFs or mutual funds only, you can skip step #4. In any case, use stop loss to protect your investment.

#Filler: The Ten Commandments of Investing.
http://www.investopedia.com/articles/basics/07/10commandments.asp
- Set goals. * Personal finances in order. * Ask questions. * Do not follow the herd. * Due diligence. * Be humble. * Be patient. * Be moderate. * No unnecessary churning. * Be safe. * Do not follow blindly.
- My additions: * Diversify. * Study market timing. * Protect your losses and profits. * Monitor your screens and your metrics. * Be emotionally detached from investments. * Learn from mistakes. * Stay away from bubbles. * Be socially responsible.

# 6    Fidelity

Fidelity offers a strong screen function. The most unique feature is incorporating its Equity Summary Score (used to be Analyst's Opinion) and some outside researches such as Zacks and Ford.

From the main menu, select "News and Research", "Screen and Filter" and then "Start a screen".

The following example selects stocks with the following criteria: Security Price (2 to 250), Market Cap. (300 and above), Equity Summary Score (8 and above), Zacks (Strongest) and Ford (Strongest).

It displays the 10 stocks. Research each stock. Read the News about each stock. You may want to use Finviz.com, Yahoo!Finance and other sources to double check.

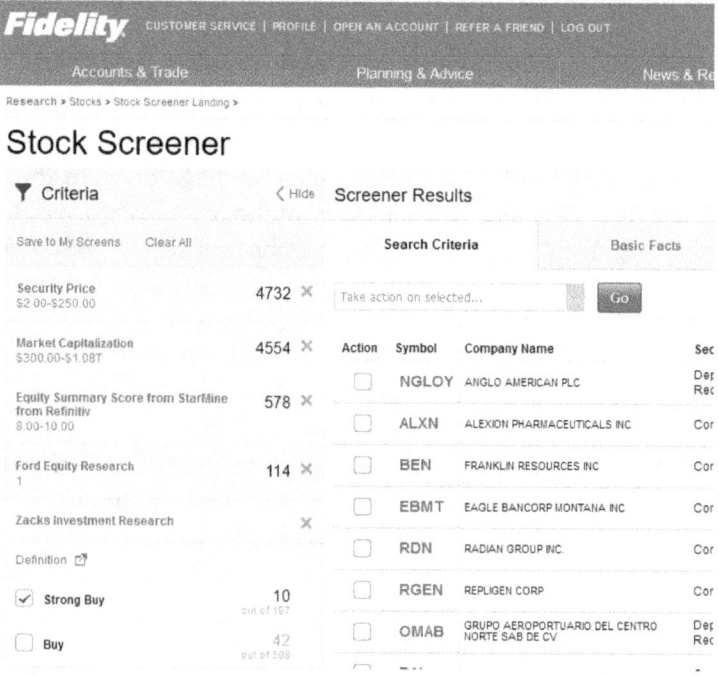

The following describes some of the features.

- Equity Summary Score. It is one of the major metrics I use in my proprietary scoring systems. They are not available to many small stocks. From my limited database in 7/2015 and for short durations, the results are:

Short Term: (7% return for the average)

| Metric | Parm. 1 | No. of Stocks | % | | Parm. 2 | No. | % | Predictability |
|---|---|---|---|---|---|---|---|---|
| Equity Summary Score | Buy | 150 | 10% | | Sell | 279 | 3% | Good |

Long Term: (8% return for the average)

| Metric | Parm. 1 | No. of Stocks | % | | Parm. 2 | No. | % | Predictability |
|---|---|---|---|---|---|---|---|---|
| Equity Summary Score | Buy | 90 | 17% | | Sell | 208 | 4% | Good |

It has its own limits, but they are very minor to me.

First, it does not have a historical database for verifying the screen performance such as the return after a year. However, I do not know any site that provides this function free. To work around this, I save the results in a spread sheet and update the performance.

Secondly, it does not provide many other filter criteria that can be found in other systems such as technical indicators or insider transactions found on Finviz.com. I use other sites for further evaluation.

Most investors should find that this screening is a very good tool and very easy to use.

# 7    The best strategy

The best-kept secret in investing is to buy a weighted ETF. I use SPY as an example here. This ETF is well diversified as it keeps all 500 stocks in the S&P 500 index. The ETF has higher position (in percentage) on stocks with higher market cap. The stocks with higher market caps usually grow the market cap by having good management and good products. The bad stocks are deleted from the index periodically.

The second best-kept secret is using simple market timing as described in this book to reduce the losses in market crashes.

It is very hard to beat this strategy. You do not need any knowledge in investing, and you only spend a few minutes every month to time the market. The market is risky when the metrics show you so such as the price is close to the simple moving average in using SMA-350 method; in this case you time the market more frequently.

# 8 Don'ts for beginners

- Do not use leverage: options, margin and leveraged ETFs.
- Do not short stocks.
- Buy low and sell high.
- Buy value stocks. Sell profitable stocks after a year and losers before holding 12 months for favorable tax treatments in non-retirement accounts. Be a turtle investor.
- Limit momentum trades.
- Use stops to protect your portfolio.
- Do not follow 'experts' blindly (most have their own agenda).
- Do not trade penny stocks (i.e. stocks less than 200 M and/or price less than $1 to my definitions).
- Venture into momentum trading when you have knowledge and time. Avoid trading systems that are available.
- Do not day trade. Most beginners lose most of their money.
- Do not take classes / seminars that promise you big money - if it works, they will give out their secrets.
- Be selective on investing subscriptions. If they give you a handful of stocks to thousands of subscribers, most likely the actual performance will not be good. Check their past performances that use real money.

# 9 Summary

The following improves the odds of success but there is no guarantee.

**Risky Market?**
Bring up Finviz.com. Enter SPY. If both SMA-50% and SMA-200% are both negative, do not invest especially when SMA-50% is more negative than SMA-200%.

## Evaluate value stocks from others' researches

Gather a list of stocks from screens and/or recommendations from magazines. Use researches that are free. Value stocks should be kept for at least 6 months. In six months or so, evaluate the bought stocks again to see whether you want to sell the stocks. Some other sites may provide free trial or one-time evaluation: IBD, GuruFocus, Zacks and Morningstar. Fidelity requires an account but there is no minimum position.

| Name | Pass Grade | Link |
|---|---|---|
| Fidelity's Equity Summary Score | >=8 | |
| Value Line[2] | Timeliness > Average | |
| | Proj. 3-5 yr.% > 5% | |
| VectorVest[1] | VST > 1 and RV > 1 | Link |
| | | |

1  Should be available from your local library.

2  Free for limited number of stocks and free trial.

## Evaluate stocks

Bring up Finviz.com and enter the stock symbol.

| Metric | Passing Grade |
|---|---|
| Forward P/E | Between 5 and 20 (25 for tech stocks) |
| P/FCF | < 15 and  ratio is positive |
| Sales Q/Q | >10 |
| EPS Q/Q | >15 |

## Intangible Analysis

Bring up Finviz, Fidelity, Yahoo!Finance or Seeking Alpha (fewer articles now) and enter the stock symbol. To prevent manipulation, the stocks should have larger cap (> 200 M) and higher daily average volume (> 10,000 shares).

## Bonus:        Simplest way to detect correction

Corrections are hard to detect, hence beginners can ignore this article for now. When the market dips temporarily, it could be the best time to buy. When the market surges temporarily, it could be the best time to sell. Get a list of value stocks to buy and have cash ready. It works great in a sideways market. However, when the market plunges, do not buy any stocks. A correction could lead to a market crash.

## How

Technical indicators may detect whether the market is ripe for temporary dips. On the average, I estimate there are two dips a year, but this number fluctuates widely. If the price is far higher than the SMA, it may be peaking for that period. RSI(14), the relative strength index using the last 14 days, determines whether the stock is overbought. It is not always reliable.

1. Bring up Finviz.com from your browser.
2. Enter SPY (an ETF simulating the S&P 500 index) on "Search Ticket".
3. SMA-200%, Single Moving Average for 200 days, indicates how far away the current stock price is from the SMA-200.
4. The market is peaking when SMA-200 is over 5%.
5. RSI(14) can be located in the right hand side of the metrics. The market is overbought when RSI(14) is over 65%.
6. When the P/E is greater than 25 (the average is 15), the market may be over-valued. Get it from http://www.multpl.com/
7. Suggested Actions:
   1. Do not buy stocks including ETFs when a correction is expected as indicated by these two conditions (#5 and #6).
   2. Do not want to exit the market totally as the market still could head higher.
   3. Sell some stocks that have reached your objectives. Do not sell more than 25% of your portfolio.
   4. Use trailing stops on the remaining stocks you bought. I recommend that you use 5% less than the current prices and 10% for volatile stocks. Adjust the stops accordingly every month.
   5. If you trade SPY or other ETFs stocks instead of stocks, skip the following.
   6. When the correction materializes and the reverse conditions occur (i.e. 5% is less than the last peak and/or RSI(14) is less than 30%), buy the ETFs and/or the stocks in your buy list.

Go back to step #1.

## Bonus:     Sample portfolio

It is a suggested sample. You need to tailor it to fit your personal requirements and your risk tolerance. In general, you should have an emergency fund for at least 3 months (6 months preferred). Many of our generation have one or even no layoff. However, I estimate the current generation will have 3 layoffs in their work life. It is due to automation, artificial intelligence, global economy, etc.

The rough estimate of stock holding in distribution between stock and bond is equal to 100 – Your Age. To illustrate in the following three portfolios, I use a 30-year old, and hence he should have 70% in stocks and 30% in bonds (including gold, CDs and cash).

In addition, some sectors are better than others according to the market conditions. The following three portfolios are for regular, todays' market and one during market crash. I use low-cost ETFs exclusively. ETF is exchange-traded funds. They are traded similar to stocks, but most are more diversified; their fees are usually lower than mutual funds.

| ETF | Normal | Today (2/2021) | Crashing[5] |
|---|---|---|---|
| SPY[1] | 40% | 30% | 0% |
| QQQ[2] | 9% | 10% | 0% |
| ARKK[2] | 1% | 0% | 0% |
| VTIAX[3] | 20% | 5% | 0% |
| LQD[3] | 15% | 20% | 5% |
| GLD | 5% | 15% | 15% |
| CD | 5% | 0% | 0% |
| Cash | 5% | 20% | 60%[6] |
| SH[4] | 0% | 0% | 5% |
| PSQ[4] | 0% | 0% | 15% |

[1] VOO is a low-fee alternative for SPY.

[2] QQQ has more tech stocks, while ARKK is active managed ETF specializing in 'disruptive technologies'. During market crashes, avoid them.

[3] VTIAX is an ETF for global companies. LQD is an ETF for corporate bonds.

[4] SH and PSQ are contra ETF to SPY and QQQ. They are shorting the corresponding index. When the market is recovering, switch them back to SPY and QQQ.

[5] Need to balance the allocations about two times a year as ETFs can grow or shrink. When the market crashes, rebalance it right away. All market will crash, and the last two (2000 and 2008) have an average loss of about 45%. Refer to the chapter "Simplest marketing timing".

[6] Today's low interest rate does not benefit us for CDs. I would leave the cash not invested and wait for the recovery to move back to stocks.

Of course, everyone's situation is different. If you are conservative, do not buy SH and PSQ. If you are afraid of inflation (especially due to the excessive printing of money), allocate more on GLD, a gold ETF.

Do not listen to financial news. They are used by institutional investors / analysts to manipulate the market. Many times they act the opposite from what they preach. This is the primary reason retail investors do not do better. With the GameStop incident, do not invest in most hedge funds. Buffett has proved the hedge funds with their high fees cannot buy an indexed ETF such as SPY.

 The above is my recommendation. In the long run, it should work fine. Consult your financial advisor before taking actions.

# Filler: Happy Mother's Day Poem
(This is my translation from a Chinese poet Yee. I made some changes due to the loss in translation.)

I cried at two unforgettable times in my life.

The first time I came to this world.
The second time you left this world.

The first time I did not know but from your mouth.
The second time you did not know but from my heart.

Between these two crises, we had endless laughs.
For the last 30 years, we had joyful laughs that had been repeated, repeated...

You treasured every laugh.
I cherish every laugh for the rest of my life.

# Section II: Screening stocks

## 1  Where the websites are

- **Free and simple screen sites**

  They are described in this article or type the following
  http://stocks.about.com/od/researchtools/a/071909screenlist.htm

  - Yahoo!Finance.
    Click here or type
    http://screener.finance.yahoo.com/stocks.html

  - Finviz.
    Click here or type
    http://Finviz.com/screener.ashx

    How to scan using Finviz (YouTube).
    https://www.YouTube.com/watch?v=aQ_0FTg9Cfw

    Screening using technical indicators (particularly useful for momentum stocks).
    https://www.YouTube.com/watch?v=RZRP2NeSX0s

  - Your broker.
    Fidelity's screens are more sophisticated than most.

  - More options: Google, CNBC.com and Moringstar.com.

  Here is a list.
  http://stocks.about.com/od/researchtools/a/071909screenlist.htm

- **Sophisticated screens (usually not free)**

  Most of them are more complicated and need time to learn. Both Vector Vest and Stock123 provide historical databases for backtesting your screens. Zacks has an earnings revision database at extra cost. GuruFocus has an easy-to-use but powerful screen function.

AAII provides screened stocks from various screens in its low-priced subscription. Both AAII and Value Line take care of some specific industries, but they provide no historical database at least for regular subscriptions. AAII provides historical performance summaries of their screens included in its subscription.

**Afterthoughts**

Here are the links to screens provided by Marketwatch and NASDAQ.
http://www.marketwatch.com/tools/stockre...
http://www.nasdaq.com/reference/stock-sc...

How to find quality stocks.
http://seekingalpha.com/article/2381395-how-to-identify-quality-stocks-and-is-there-really-alpha-to-be-had

# Filler
"Sell in May" could be a self-fulfilled prophecy. I prefer to sell on April 1 and come back on Oct. 15 to avoid the herd.

## 2    Finviz.com screener

You should use fundamental metrics for fundamental stocks, growth metrics for growth stocks, momentum metrics for momentum stocks, or a combination. Basically you want to keep the fundamental stocks longer so the market would realize their values.

Finviz.com provides a screening function incorporating both fundamental and technical metrics and is one of the best free sites. Bring up Finviz.com in your browser and select screener. You have 4 tabs: Descriptive, Fundamental, Technical and All. It has the following features:

- The criteria specified can be saved but the number is limited.
- The searched stocks can be saved in a portfolio (for paper trading and performance monitoring).
- Technical indicators.
- For an extra fee, you can have a historical database. This would help you to test your strategies. The historical database is quite limited for some technical parameters only.
- Some advanced technical indicators work well especially useful in momentum trading.
- Use technical patterns. My favorites are Head and Shoulder and Double Bottoms (Peaks).
- Combine fundamental metrics and technical metrics to narrow down your selection.
- Combine fundamental metrics and technical metrics to narrow down your selection.
- Add Insider Trans (> 5% for me), Short Squeeze (> 20%), etc. for specific purposes.
- Candlesticks is hard to master. You need to read a book dedicated to it.

http://www.investopedia.com/terms/c/candlestick.asp
https://www.youtube.com/watch?v=FsqoV1aVrUc&list=WL&index=56

Finviz's screener lacks the following features:

- Stocks with prices trending up in the last several weeks (such as increasing X% in the previous week).

- Using exponential moving averages that supposedly have better predictive power than simple moving averages for momentum investing.
- Selecting ranges such as selecting all three major exchanges and market cap ranges.
- P/E for an ETF. It can be obtained from other sources such as ETFdb.com.
- When the earnings (E) is negative, you may have the wrong values for P/E and the metrics using E. For example, if you want stocks with P/E less than 20, the screener returns you stocks with negative earnings.
- Combine fundamental metrics and technical metrics to narrow down your selection.

All of these missing features can be worked around. The paid version may provide better functions.

**Links:**

Investopedia.
http://www.investopedia.com/university/features-of-Finviz-elite/other-chart-features.asp

How to scan using Finviz (YouTube).
https://www.YouTube.com/watch?v=aQ_0FTg9Cfw
https://www.youtube.com/watch?v=tHtovnCY6uY&list=WL&index=96
(Recommended)

Finviz's screener tutorial.
https://www.youtube.com/watch?v=glMtwB7OVf4&list=WL&index=56

Swing trading
https://www.youtube.com/watch?v=M8sNMhPJINU&list=WL&index=55

Screening using technical indicators (YouTube).
https://www.YouTube.com/watch?v=RZRP2NeSX0s

A screener example

The following is an example. Fine tune the selection criteria according to your personal criteria and risk tolerance.

- Bring up Finviz.com from your browser. Select Screener, the third tab. As of 3/24/2015, we have 7066 stocks.

- For illustration purposes, we would like to find stocks with double bottoms, a positive technical indicator. Select the Technical tab. Select Pattern and then Double Bottom. Now we have 257 stocks.

- Select the Fundamental tab that is next to the Technical tab. Select Forward P/E and then select "under 20". Now, we have 86 stocks.

- Select Debt/Equity less than .5. Now, we have 45 stocks. Some industries such as utilities are traditionally high in debt, so you can use 'less than 1'.

- Select EPS growth Q-to-Q over 10%. Now, we have 19 stocks.

- Select the Description tab. Select Country to USA. Now, we have 17 stocks.

- Select Price > 1. Select Avg. Volume "Over 100K". Select Float Short "Under 10%. Select Analyst Recs. "Buy or better". Now we have 9 stocks.

  Now we can evaluate them one by one using Fundamental Analysis, Intangible Analysis, Qualitative Analysis and Technical Analysis. The purpose of screening is to filter the 7000 stocks to a small number (9 stocks in this case).

Skip the stocks that have the Earnings Date within 2 weeks. If you already have too many stocks in the same industry, skip that stock. You can save the screen when you have registered with Finviz.com. It is free. Check the performance of your selections after 3 months or so.

## Common parameters

Different styles of investing use different parameters for screening stocks. Here is my suggested parameters in using Finviz.com. Vary them to your risk tolerance and market conditions. Finviz.com is not complete in all functions, but it could the best free screener that incorporates both the fundamental and the technical criteria. The first table is for Value and the next one for Growth. The last one is for finding stocks that the institutional investors are trading.

## Screening value stocks

| Value Screens | Common | Penny | Micro Cap | Dividend |
|---|---|---|---|---|
| **General** | | | | |
| Market Cap (M) | >500 M | <50 M | 50 -200 M | +Mid(>2B) |
| Price | >5 | < 5 | 1-15 | >5 |
| In all 3 Exchanges | In | Not In | Most are In | In |
| Avg. Volume | >100K | >5K | >10K | >100K |
| Country | USA | USA | USA | USA |
| Dividend% | | | | >3% |
| Float Short | <10% | <10% | <10% | <10% |
| Analyst Rec | Buy or + | Buy or + if avail. | Buy or + | Buy or + |
| | | | | |
| **Fundamental** | | | | |
| Forward P/E | <20 | <20 | <20 | <25 |
| ROE | >10 | >10 | >5 | >15 |
| QQ earning | >0 | | | >0 |
| QQ sales | >0 | | | >0 |
| PEG | <1 | <1 | <1 | <1.2 |
| Payout% | | | | 20-50% |
| P/S | <10 | <10 | <10 | <10 |
| | | | | |
| **Technical** | | | | |
| Price above 200 SMA | Yes | Yes | Yes | Yes |
| RSI(14) | < 70 | < 70 | < 70 | < 70 |

There may be no analysts or very few following penny stocks and micro-cap stocks. QQ is quarter to quarter.

## Screening Growth Stocks

| Growth Screen | Common | Technical | Momentum |
|---|---|---|---|
| **General** | | | |
| Market Cap (M) | >50 | > 1,000 | >500 |
| Price | >1 | >10 | >5 |
| Exchanges (Major 3) | In | In | In |
| Avg. Volume | >50K | >200K | >100K |
| | | | |
| **Fundamental** | | | |
| Forward P/E | <30 | <30 | <30 |
| Return of Equity | >5 | >0 | >0 |
| QQ earning | >10% | >15% | >20% |
| QQ sales | >5% | > 5% | >10% |
| PEG | <1 | <1 | <1 |
| Analyst recs. | Buy or + | | |
| | | | |
| **Technical** | | | |
| Price above 200 SMA | Yes | Yes | |
| 50  SMA | Yes | Yes | Yes |
| RSI | < 75 | < 75 | |

Short-term trends are important for momentum stocks.

## Explanation

The above are suggestions only. Adjust them to your personal preferences and risk tolerance.

- Finviz screener lacks ranges, such as market cap and multiple of exchanges. Most Finviz's parameters do not have a range option such as Exchanges, so you need to run the screen three times, one for each of the three major exchanges.

- Average Volume. When the price of the stock is less than $3, double the average volume requirement. In most cases, 10K is quite acceptable to me. When the volume is small, you may have to pay more (a.k.a. spread) to trade.

- There are many fundamental metrics such as Debt/Equity and Price/Free Cash Flow that are not included here, but they should be included in your further evaluation. Each industry sector has different thresholds. For example, the P/S is very different for a supermarket rather than a high-tech company. Compare the company to the average value of the companies in the same sector. Many sites including GuruFocus.com and Fidelity.com have the average values displayed.

- For momentum stock, you can ignore most of the fundamentals and concentrate on the price trend such as SMA-20% (Simple Moving Average for the last 20 trade sessions) and SMA-50%. The higher the percent, the higher it is away from its own average. You do not want to hold momentum stocks too long (max. 3 months unless the momentum is still uptrend); personally my max. is 1 month.

- For growth stocks, ensure the PEG (P/E growth), quarter-to-quarter earnings and quarter-to-quarter sales are above the averages in its own sector and/or the market.

- Technical analysis favors large cap stocks with large volumes. I prefer stocks with positive earnings and they are fundamentally sound.

- When the SMA-20%, SMA-50% and SMA-200% are all positive, they should be in an uptrend.

- RSI(14) indicates whether the stock is oversold (>65) or under bought (<30). The range is my suggestion only.

- You may want to check out your strategies using a virtual account from your broker.

**A general guideline for Institutional investors**

| Criteria | Value |
| --- | --- |
| Description | |
|    Relative Volume | Over 2 M |
|    Country | USA usually |
|    Institution Ownership | Over 50% |
| | |
| Technical | |
|    SMA-200 | >10% |
|    Volatility | Week – Over 3% |
|    RSI(14) | >40% |
| | |
| Fundamental | |

| Market Cap | >1B |
|------------|------|
| ROE | >10% |

- Again, these are my suggested metrics. I prefer USA companies and many are global companies. If you use foreign countries, ensure they are larger companies and/or in countries that have regulations similar to our SEC's.
- For value investors, select Forward P/E less than 20 (25 for high-tech companies) and their Earnings are positive.
- Check out how many analysts are following the stocks that you are interested in.

To illustrate, I find 12 stocks. I narrow them down to 3. First, I skip all stocks that already have had more than 10% rise recently. They may have risen too high already.

Select profitable stocks with forward P/E less than 25. "Debt/Equity" is less than .5 (50%). Then, ROI is higher than 25%. Stop when you have reached the optimal number of stocks (3 for me in this example).

If you find too many stocks, tighten the criteria and vice versa. Save the criteria and the selected stocks in a portfolio for paper trading.

# Filler: Irresponsible is my best defense

I told my date that I would not be responsible after the second drink due to the lack of an enzyme.

---

# Filler
Starbucks is being sued for too many ice cubes in the ice coffee. If he wins, he would sue MacDonald's, Burger King... and be a billionaire. Why did I not think of this? The lady won for the spilling of hot coffee. The jury did not know that eventually we had to pay for all of these and made the lawyers rich. Too many unproductive lawyers makes it tough to operate a business including small businesses. In many countries besides the U.S., the one who sues and loses has to pay for court expenses.

---

# 3    Fidelity

Fidelity offers a strong screen function. The most unique feature is incorporating its Equity Summary Score (used to be Analyst's Opinion) and some outside researches such as Zacks and Ford.

From the main menu, select "News and Research", "Screen and Filter" and then "Start a screen".

The following example selects stocks with the following criteria: Security Price (2 to 250), Market Cap. (300 and above), Equity Summary Score (8 and above), Zacks (Strongest) and Ford (Strongest).

It displays the 10 stocks. Research each stock. Read the News about each stock. You may want to use Finviz.com, Yahoo!Finance and other sources to double check.

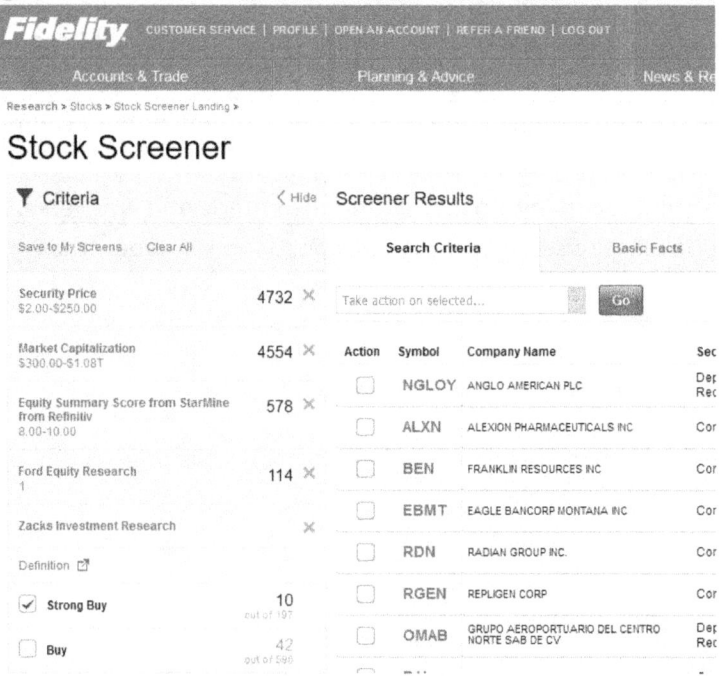

The following describes some of the features.

- Equity Summary Score. It is one of the major metrics I use in my proprietary scoring systems. They are not available to many small stocks. From my limited database in 7/2015 and for short durations, the results are:

Short Term: (7% return for the average)

| Metric | Parm. 1 | No. of Stocks | % | | Parm. 2 | No. | % | Predictability |
|---|---|---|---|---|---|---|---|---|
| Fidelity Analyst | Buy | 150 | 10% | | Sell | 279 | 3% | Good |

Long Term: (8% return for the average)

| Metric | Parm. 1 | No. of Stocks | % | | Parm. 2 | No. | % | Predictability |
|---|---|---|---|---|---|---|---|---|
| Fidelity Analyst | Buy | 90 | 17% | | Sell | 208 | 4% | Good |

It has its own limits, but they are very minor to me.

First, it does not have a historical database for verifying the screen performance such as the return after a year. However, I do not know any site that provides this function free. To work around this, I save the results in a spread sheet and update the performance.

Secondly, it does not provide many other filter criteria that can be found in other systems such as technical indicators or insider transactions found on Finviz.com. I use other sites for further evaluation.

Most investors should find that this screening is a very good tool and very easy to use.

# Section III: Pick stocks for appreciation

After the market is not risky (Section I) and we have picked up stocks (Section II), we still need to evaluate the stocks. Most stocks with bad fundamentals will not appreciate. However there are examples on turnaround situations (some call them catalysts) such as:

- A new drug has positive test result.
- A new product.
- A new discovery or breakthrough.
- Being acquired.
- Being settled with a major lawsuit.

Screen stocks first and then analyze the screened stocks one by one.

The most updated information is from the Earning Conference Call (easier to obtain it from SeekingAlpha), Q10 report and from the company's website. Finviz.com seems to be more updated than most other sites besides the above.

When to sell a stock? I have three chapters at the end of this section. They are in the same topic but in different approaches / concepts.

The better analysis gives you better chance of success, but as everything in life there is no guarantee.

# 4      Finviz's parameters

Most metrics are described in Finviz (via Help), Investopedia and/or Wikipedia and my chapter on P/E. The following are my personal comments and why I feel some metrics are more important than others. Compare the ratios to the companies in the same sector and also its averages from the last 5 years.

From your browser, enter Finviz.com. Enter a symbol (I used ABEO for discussion). A chart is displayed with the prices and volumes for the last nine months. SMAs (Single Moving Average) are displayed sometimes with other technical indicators. Intraday, Daily and Weekly options are available.

Besides the metrics described next and the chart, it describes what the company does, analysts' recommendations (I prefer Fidelity's Equity Summary), insiders' trading and articles that are good for qualitative analysis. "Financial Highlights and Statements" are materials for more in-depth analysis and they were more important decades ago when most financial ratios had not been calculated for you.

The following metrics are roughly based on the flow of Finviz from top to bottom and left to right. I skip those metrics that I believe are not too important. You can also place your cursor on the metric to have the description from Finviz. Some metrics are left blank to indicate they are not applicable (zero, negative or not available). For example, the Debt/Equity of YRCW in 1/2019 is blank (same as null) due to Equity being negative. From Yahoo!Finance, it has a total debt of 888M.

- **Index**. Most of us trade stocks in the three major exchanges in the USA. Stocks listed in over-the-counter are too risky for most of us. Skip the stocks in local exchanges and foreign exchanges if you are not an expert on these stocks. I screen the stocks and then ignore the stocks that are not in the Dow, NASDAC and Amex. Other screeners may let you to select a group of exchanges.

- **Market Cap** (MC). To me, stocks below 50M are risky even they could be very profitable. Ensure the Avg. Volume is at least 10,000 shares and / or your order is less than 1% of the average volume. Some small stocks are controlled by the owners and have small volumes. In this case you cannot sell your stock easily.

Float = Outstanding shares – Insider shares.

Usually it does not matter as they are typically the same. However, it does for small companies with large insider shares. Most of these owners do not want to sell their family businesses and hence they reduce the chance of being acquired entirely or partially for good prices.

- If **Forward P/E** (a.k.a. Expected P/E) is not provided, use the P/E which is based on the trailing last 12 months (TTM). Alternatively, calculate the E by using the E from P/E and multiplying it by its growth rate. It may not be seasonally adjusted. I prefer Expected P/E (or called Forward P/E) as it provides a better predictability power from my limited research.

  Finviz.com leaves the P/E blank (same as null) if the earnings are negative. In this case, I would check out Yahoo!Finance's EV / EBITDA, which also considers taxes and interests. It is similar to the blank on some metrics, if the Asset is negative even they seldom occur.

  Earnings Yield is equal to E/P and True Earnings Yield (my term) is EBITDA / EV. It is easier to understand. Compare it to the annual dividend yield of a 10-year Treasury which is quite safe. It is also useful in screening and sorting the screened stocks. If you use P/E instead of E/P, in most cases you need to screen or sort stocks with a clause "P/E > 0".

  Compare the P/E or Forward P/E with the average P/E for the sector and its average P/E for the last 5 years that are available from Fidelity.com. Some sectors have high P/Es. If the sector is cyclical, the earnings could be affected.

- **Cash / share**. It is used to calculate Pow P/E and Pow EY when EV/EBITDA is not available. To illustrate, if the stock is $10 and it has $10 cash / share without debt (i.e. Debt/Equity = 0), most likely it is underpriced as you can get the whole company for nothing. You should find out why the price is so low. It could be the market ignoring the stock, or there is a serious event happening such as major lawsuit.

- **Dividend %** is useful for income investors. The payout ratio should not be more than 30% except for matured companies.

- **Recs**. Select stocks with 1 or 2. Do not base your stock selection on this recommendation alone. There have been many bad recommendations that could cost you a fortune in losses. Use Fidelity's Equity Summary Score instead.

- **PEG** is a measure of the growth of P/E and hence a growth metric. The lower value is better as long as earnings are positive. If earnings are negative, then the reverse is true. It is a defect in using P/E and PEG and that's why I recommend EY (Earnings Yield) and EYG, earnings yield growth.

   If there are two companies with the same P/E, the one with a better PEG ratio is better. If two companies have the same E/P, the company with higher Earnings Growth (EPS Q/Q) would be better.

- **P/B**. Book value (= Total Assets – Total Liabilities) may not include intangible asset such as patents. Do not trust it 100%, so is ROE which is based on book value. Negative equity is possible when Total Liabilities is more than Total Assets.

- **P/S**. If two companies are unprofitable, this ratio can be used. I prefer profitable companies.

- **P/FCF**. I prefer it to be greater than 0 and less than 50 for value investors. Most metrics can be manipulated easily, but not this one.

- **Sales Q/Q** reduces the seasonal deviation. To illustrate, retail sales for the Christmas season should be compared it to the same season in prior year.

- **EPS Q/Q**. Same as above. I prefer the growth of EPS over Sales. Both of these Q/Q ratios are growth metrics. When a company terminates its unprofitable product(s), its Sales Q/Q could be down but its EPS Q/Q could be up. In 2000, many internet companies had great Sales Q/Qs but negative EPS Q/Qs.

   Q/Q comparison (quarter to quarter) takes out the seasonal variations.

When the company buys its own shares, EPS could be misleading as E is fixed and the number of shares is reduced. In most cases, the fundamentals of the company has not changed.

- Positive **Insider** Transactions are favorable. Sometimes, they are misleading. Need to scroll to the end of the screen and check out more info there. If the transactions are outdated such as 3 months or so ago, and or they are buys in a similar amount than the sells a while ago, they are not important. Insiders know the company better than us. So is Institutional Transactions as institutional investors move the market.

- Insider Own, Shares Outstanding and Shares **Float** determine the number of shares that are available for trading. A small Float with a high Insider Own limits trading and the stock should be avoided in most cases. Compare your trade position for the stock to the Avg. Volume.

- **Profit Margin**. I prefer it over Gross Margin and Oper. Margin which does not include interest expenses and taxes. When you sell software, the Gross Margin is high as it does not include development, support and marketing, etc. A retail store has low Gross Margin. It all depends on the industry, and hence it is better to compare companies in the same industry.

- **Short Float**. I prefer it to be less than 10%. If it is greater than 10%, the shorters could find something wrong with the company. If it is over 25%, I would check the fundamentals. If they are good, I would buy expecting a short squeeze potential. It has been risky but proven to be profitable for me.

- Technical metrics: SMA-20, SMA-50 and SMA-200. Finviz expresses them in convenient percentages. If they are all positive, it means the trend is up. SMA-20 is short-term trend and SMA-200 is a long-term trend. If you are short-term swing investor, stick with short-term trend and vice versa. The first two are momentum grades. Many long-term investors do not buy stocks when their SMA-200% is negative.

- **RSI(14)**. If it greater than 65%, it is overbought. If it is under 30%, it is under bought for me. Some use 5% up or down than mine. Use it as a reference. Most stocks making new heights are always overbought, and many of these stocks keep on rising. I recommend use trailing stops to protect your profit.

- **Beta**. A volatile stock fluctuates a lot. It is good for short-term traders. A beta of 1 means the stock would fluctuate with the market and more volatile if it is higher than 1. For volatile stocks (higher than 1), the stops should be higher. For example, if your stops are normally 5%, you may want to use 7% or even higher.

- Management performance is measured by <u>ROE</u>. It is also judged by **Analysts' Rec.** and Institutional Ownership (except for small companies). The confidence of their own ability, the company and its sector is measured by Insider Ownership and Insider Purchases.

  ROE = Net Income / Average Shareholder's Equity
  According to Investopedia, a normal ROE for utilities should be 10% while high tech companies should be 15%. Compare this ration and many other ratios with its peers that is available from Fidelity.
- Avoid all bankrupting companies at all cost. Debt/Equity, P/FCF, Cash/Sh., P/B, Profit Margin, Forward P/E, Short Float, RSI(14), SMA20% and SMA50 would give us hints. Need to summarize all the info and study many other factors such as obsoleting products (including drugs).
- Unless you have concrete information, do not buy stocks a week or so before the Earnings Date.

More useful information:
- The price chart. It has a lot of features such as the resistance line. Some charts include technical indicators such as double top (a bearish warning) and double bottom (a bullish sign).
- Description under the symbol. It briefly describes what the company (sector and industry) does and its country of registration. You want to buy a stock within a sector that is trending up. For example according to Finviz, Apple is in the Consumer Goods sector and the Electronic Equipment industry.

  If you do not want to buy foreign stocks, skip it if it is not listed in the US exchange.
- Articles on the company for qualitative analysis.
- Insider trading. Pay more attention to the insider purchases at market prices. Use common sense.
- The last line lets you open Yahoo!Finance and other sites.

## Your broker's website

Your broker website should have plenty of tools to analyze stocks. As of Dec., 2018, Fidelity lets you use their extensive research free by opening an account with no position restriction. I describe some of their metrics that should be beneficial to your research.

- Equity Summary Score. Potentially good buy when it is 7 (8 for conservative investors) or higher. With some exceptions, you should avoid or short stocks if the score is 3 or below. The stocks ranking from 4 to 6 could be turnaround candidates if they are supported by good Q/Q Earnings and/or good news.

- The 5-year averages are good yardsticks. For example, in Dec., 2018, C's P/E is about 9 and the average is 14. Hence it is a value buy.

## 5      Intangibles

I give a score for each stock I evaluate. Occasionally some stocks with poor scores have great returns and vice versa. In general, the scoring system works. It has been proven statistically and repeatedly from my limited data. I stick with high-score stocks with some exceptions.

Once in a while I change my scoring system to adept to the current market conditions. To illustrate, the market bottom phase and early recovery phase of the market cycle favor value more than momentum/growth. Here are some of my recent experiences and strategies:

- I double or even triple my stake on stocks with high scores. In the longer term, they are consistently better winners than the average with some minor exceptions. Besides the score, look at the intangibles described in this article.

- Watch out for the stocks with outrageous metrics such as P/E of 4 or less. It could be a big lawsuit pending, an expiration of some important drugs, etc. Also, be careful with scores in the top 5%. From my statistics they do worse than the average. Their problems may not show up in the current financial statements.

- The technology of a tech company cannot be ignored even though the company's P/E is high, that I set a limit of 25 instead of 20 for other stocks. The value of the company's technology and patents will not be shown in the fundamental metrics except from the insiders' purchases at market prices.

For example, IDCC rose about 40% in 2 days. There was a rumor that Google was buying the company and/or Apple was bidding on it too for its mobile technology. Charts usually would flag this kind of event. For non-charters, use the SMA-20% from Finviz.com. They could be a little late as the charts depend on rising prices.

- There are more acquisitions during a market bottom (same as early recovery). The companies with good technologies are bargains and the larger companies especially those in the same sector understand their values better than most of us. These potentially profitable companies will not be shown by their scores explicitly. When corporations have a lot of cash or the credit is cheap, they are looking for smaller companies to acquire or invest in. The candidates are usually small, beaten up, low-priced and having valuable intangible assets such as technologies, customer base and/or market share of the industry segment. 2009-2012 was just the perfect environment and the before that was 2003. I had at least one stock in each of these periods and they appreciated a lot.

- The opposite is Netflix, Chipotle in 1/2012 and Amazon in 1/2013. They are overpriced by any measure. However, the mentioned companies are investing in the future. The shorters (not for beginners) are having a tough time in making money on them. When their P/Es are higher than 40, watch out. Some could be OK in the mentioned companies, but usually they are not. Do not follow the herd and your due diligence will verify whether they will still go up.

Use reward/risk ratio. It is based on experiences. To illustrate, if the company has the equal chance to go up 50% and go down 25%, then it is a buy and the reverse is a sell.

- The retail investor just cannot possibly know about some events until they actually happen. For example, ATSC dropped 15% due to losing its second primary customer. Fundamentals cannot predict this kind of events. Charts can signal this event, but usually they are too late unless you watch the chart all day long.

- After a quick run up, TZOO plunged due to missing some negligible earning expectations. It seems the original climbing prices already had the perfect earnings growth built-in.

  I do not understand why a company loses 10% of its market cap when it missed by 1% of the expected earnings. It could be driven up and down by the institutional investors. Evaluate the stock before you act. Acting opposite to the institutional investors could be very profitable for the right stocks. Avoid trading before the earnings announcement dates (about 4 times a year for most stocks).

- The following are not easily found in financial statements: industry outlook, patents, good will, market share, competition, product margins, management quality, lawsuits pending, potential acquisition, pension obligations, advertising icons, etc. That is why we need to read articles on the stocks in our buy list or our purchased stocks.

- The financial data could be fraudulent or manipulated. I do not trust small companies in emerging markets. I have been burned too many times. Check the company names such as foreign names, ADR and their headquarter addresses (from the company profile in most investing sites).

  Earnings can be manipulated with many accounting tricks. A jump in earnings from last year may not be as rosy as it looks. Check the footnotes in the accounting statements. I usually skip financial statements unless I have big purchases in mind as my time in investing is limited.

- Cash flow cannot be easily manipulated. It is good information whether the company will survive or not, but to me it does not prove to be a consistent predictor in my tests, but an important red flag for companies on their way to bankruptcy. Examples abound.

- Repeated one-time, non-recurring and extraordinary charges are red flags.

- Stay away from the companies where the CEOs are over-compensated. As of 7- 2013, Activision's CEO raised his salary by more than 600%, while the stock lost its value in double digits.

- Value stocks. Need to know why they become value stocks (i.e. fewer investors want to own) even they are financially sound. For example, there are two primary reasons for the downfall of a supplier to Apple: 1. Apple is declining in sales and 2. Apple is switching suppliers to replace their product. Technology companies are continually building better mouse traps. They could turn around in a year or so with better products.

## Conclusion

Buying a stock is an educated guess that its stock price will rise. Fundamentals do not always work, but they work most of the time:

1. When we buy a value stock, we're swimming against the tide. Hence, we need to wait longer (usually more than 6 months) for the market to realize its value. The exception is the Early Recovery phase (see the Market Cycle chapter) and it has faster and larger returns than most other stocks from most other stages of the market cycle.

2. Some metrics are misleading. Book value could be misleading for an established company such as IBM. The image of the cowboy in a tobacco company could be a very important asset that is not included in its financial statement.

3. The market is not always rational.

## Afterthoughts

- Brand names of big companies are one of the most important intangibles. Here is a strategy to buy big companies in a down market. It has been proven that it works. However, do not just buy these companies without analysis.
  http://seekingalpha.com/article/1324041-buying-brand-names-in-a-bear-market-can-make-you-rich

- The reputation of a company takes a long time to build but a bad incidence to destroy in the case of GM such as the delay in recalling the killer switches.

# 6      Qualitative analysis

This is the last analysis to evaluate a stock fundamentally. Then the next is technical analysis which is used to find an entry point (also the exit point) for the stock.

**Where quantitative analysis fails and why**

I find that some stocks with high scores fail and some stocks with low scores succeed as indicated by my performance monitor. The scoring system still works statistically for the majority of my stocks.

- Reasons why stocks with low scores perform in addition to the described in the last discussion:

  o Oversold. The institutional investors (fund managers and pension managers) dump them first, and then followed by the retail investors. These big boys will buy these stocks back when they reach a certain price range. RSI(14), a technical indicator described in the Technical Analysis article, is useful to detect these oversold stocks. This metric is readily available from many sites including Finviz.

  o The falling price (P) improves all fundamental metrics that have the stock price such as P/E and P/Sales. However, the trend of the price is down.

  o The company has turned around after fixing its problems and/or the market has changed for the better.

  o The current problems have been resolved but not known to the public. It includes resolving a lawsuit, a new product, a new drug, or a new big order, etc.

  o Heavy purchases by insiders. The company's outlook is not shown in its financial statements. Sometimes the insiders hide them so they can buy more of their companies' stocks for themselves.

- Reasons why stocks with high scores plunge in addition to the described in the previous discussion:

- o The company's fundamentals and its prices have reached or closed to the maximum heights. They have no way to go but down. It is particularly true when the stock's timing rating is at or close to the highest point. TTWO that I gifted to my grandchildren had been 5-baggers in the last few years before it plunged in 2018.

- o It has reached its potential value (or a target price) and it is time for many investors to take profits.

- o Sector (or stock) rotation, particularly by institutional investors who drive the market.

- o The outlook of the company, its sector and/or the market is deteriorating.

- o The stock price may be manipulated. There are many reasons to pump and dump the stock. Shorting is not recommended for most investors. However, some experienced shorters make money consistently when they find valid reasons to short stocks.

- o It could be due to a new serious lawsuit, a new competing product or drug, canceling a major order, etc.

- o Downgrade by analysts. They could spot some bad events such as product defects, violations of regulations or accounting errors / frauds. The downgrades are more important than the upgrades that could have conflict of interest.

- o The financial statement had been manipulated. The SEC may ask for an investigation.

- o Does not meet the consensus in earnings announcements, which have been over-acted by many investors.

**Qualitative Analysis**

We need to do further analysis after the quantitative analysis and the intangible analysis. Check out the company's prospects. Check out the date of the article and any potential hidden agenda items from the author. Older articles may not have much value.

Be careful on 'pump-and-dump' manipulation written by authors with a hidden agenda. It has happened especially on small companies before even SeekingAlpha.com has its share. Here was an article that tells you to sell NHTC. There was another article to tell you to buy ARTX. They fit into this category.

The sources are:

1.  Seeking Alpha.
    Type the symbol of the company to read as many articles on the company as you have time for. Today this site and many other similar sites require you to be a paid member. If you cannot find too many good articles, check out the articles from Finviz.com.

    Recently, I read an article on AMD and it said it may have good profits in the next two years with the game consoles. The outlook of a company is not shown by any fundamental metric which are far from favorable.

    Following a well-known writer, I bought IBM without doing my due diligence (my fault). It went down more than 15% quickly. You can learn from my mistakes.

2.  Research reports from your broker. If you do not find many, open an account with one that provides such reports. Some subscription services such as Value Line provide such reports.

3.  Yahoo!Finance board. Most comments are garbage. However, once in a while you find some great insights. Usually you cannot find any info from other sources on tiny companies.

4.  The most recent company's financial statements. They are usually available in the company's website.

5.  10-Ks from Edgar database (www.sec.gov/edgar). Check out new products and its potential competition, key customers, order backlog, research and development and pending lawsuits.

6.  Check out the outlook of the sector the company is in and the company itself.

7. Check out its competitors.

8. Some companies are run by stupid people. I received information via my email saying that my mutual fund account could be treated as an abandoned property. I have been cashing dividend checks every year and why it would be considered as an abandoned property. I called them right away to close my account.

   The tall and handsome guy presented articulately how he would turn around JC Penny on TV. I could tell you right away that all his tricks had been tried by other companies such as Sears, and most did not work. The intelligent investor does not care about how handsome, how articulated, how rich his family is and how many advanced degrees from prestigious colleges he possesses. If he does not make sense, do not buy his preaching and his company's stock. [Update. As of 5/2020, J.C. Penny filed for bankruptcy protection. If you had this stock and my book, you would have saved a lot of money minus $10 for my book!]

9. Check out its business model. Some business models do not make business sense and some do. Here are some samples.

- Giving razors makes sense, as the customers have to buy the blades eventually and keep on buying blades for life.

- Supermarket M lowers prices on common merchandises such as Coke and it works. They make money by providing inferior (but profitable to them) products that you cannot compare prices easily such as meat and seafood.

  Eventually there will be a supermarket in my area to satisfy me both in price and quality or at least make a good tradeoff.

- Last week it had been brutally hot. I went to a Barns & Noble's bookstore to enjoy reading the updated books and enjoyed the air conditioning. When there are more free loaders like me than customers, this business model does not work.

- Market dumping works to capture the market. Microsoft used to do it with their new Office and Mail products that could not compete with the established products at the time.

# 7    Avoid bankrupting companies

Avoid the bankrupting companies at all costs. Here are some hints that a company is going bankrupt:

- I had several companies that had lost most of their stock values. It turns out that most were Chinese companies. I did have some losers from Mexico, Israel and Ireland. I believe most were set up to cheat investors. Most if not all had 'rosy' financial statements. Avoid them, especially small companies in emerging countries.

- Many U.S. companies failed due to fraud, poor management, and/or the management betting wrongly. When the CEO is using the company as his own AMT, or having an extravagant life style, watch out. If they promise you a return doubling the current rate of return of the market, listen to your wise mother: there is no free lunch. Despite so many real examples, still fools are born every day, because greed is a human nature.

- Do not follow the 'commentators' on TV. They have their own hidden agenda which usually is not in your interest.

- Many companies fail due to their lack of ability to pay back their loans. Except for specific industries and situations, avoid companies with high debt (Debt/Equity over 50%). Financial institutions and companies that have high debt in order to finance their products for their customers such as utilities are the exceptions.

- I have a screen named Big Losers beating the market by more than 600% in Early Recovery (a phase defined by me). However, some bankrupted companies are not included in the database which is termed as survivor bias. Hence, the actual result is far worse than the 600%. I still use this screen but skip these companies using the following yardsticks.
    - The companies are usually safe with high Free Cash Flow / Equity and high Expected Profit / Stock Price.
    - The following are red flags: low Free Cash Flow / Equity, high Inventory and high Receivable (esp. relative to its Payable), high P/B (over 30) and high net Debt/Equity (over 1 to 3 depending on the industry).
    - P/PFC should be greater than 0 and less than 50. A healthy cash flow may not be able to service the debt if it is too huge. Hence, compare it to Debt/Equity. Compare the cash flow per year to debt obligations per year.

- New government regulations could bankrupt an industry. What would happen when the U.S. takes out the rebates and subsidies of solar panels? When the U.S. banned solar panels from China, one of my Chinese stocks went bankrupt. Also government bailed out bankrupting companies such as Chrysler (that I made a good profit) and AIG Fannie Mae in 2008.

- Serious lawsuits- Most U.S. companies are required to file this information in their financial reports.
- Obsolete products. Newspapers, retail and similar products would be replaced by the internet. The opposite is new products such as virtual reality products.
- Many companies run out of money during the development phase of the major products. Many are too optimistic in their business plans.
- If you expect the market will recover in 2 years, ensure the company's cash and net income can support their burn rate for at least two more years.
- Many investing sites (most require subscriptions) have safety scores.
- If the Beneish M-Score is greater than -2.22, the company is likely an accounting manipulator.
- Choose companies with Z-Score higher than 3; it does not applicable to financial companies. Both M-Score and Z-Score are available from GuruFocus, a paid subscription. Z-Score does not work for financial institutions.
- Z-Score metrics are: "Working Capital / Total Assets" (A), "Retained Earnings / Total Assets" (B), "Earnings Before Interest & Taxes / Total Assets" (C), "Market Cap / Total Liabilities" (D) and "Sales / Total Assets" (E).
  Z-Score = 1.2 A + 1.4 B + 3.3 C +.6 D + E
- Market timing- It does not always work, but it is far better to follow a proven technique than not. It is far safer to take money out of the market when the market is too risky or is plunging. The big losers are companies that provide non-essential products in a down turn.
- Small companies could be risky but very profitable. Typically they have a low stock price (less than $5), small market cap (less than 50 M), low sales (less than $25 M) and low institutional ownership (less than 5%).
- Avoid companies when their own bond ratings are not equal to AAA or AA (www.moodys.com).
- The fall of a sector such as oil in 2015 could drive the related companies, or even a country to the brink of bankruptcy.

Investing is risky to start with. However, investing especially in stocks has been proven to be the best vehicle to beat inflation.

## 8    *When to sell a stock*

There are many reasons to sell a stock as follows.

**Personal**

1.  Has met my targets/objectives.
    It could be a 10% gain in a very short-term swing, x% return in 4 months for a short-term swing or y% gain after a year for long-term trades. Define x and y depending on your risk tolerance and how often you trade.

    I bought 4 stocks in one day during the August, 2015 correction and placed sell orders with 10% more than my purchase prices. I sold one in a day and another one within a month. This is my strategy for correction – sometimes it works and sometimes it does not.

    Never look back. Do not blame yourself when the prices are better than your trade prices. When the market is volatile, use a higher percent of the current prices. Be disciplined. Stay on the same strategy and detach yourself from emotions.

2.  Realize that we have made a mistake. Do not let your ego block your eyes. It could be due to bad analysis, bad, data, unexpected fraud, lawsuits, and/or unforeseeable events that you have no control of. It is better to get out with a small loss. I prefer a 25% loss as a threshold for long-term strategies and a 10% (or less for some strategies) loss for short-term strategies.

    We have to ensure whether it is a mistake or not. If the 'mistake' is just bad luck or due to conditions we cannot possibly predict or control, then it is not a mistake. If it is a mistake, learn from it. When we diversify, one bad loss should not cause a big dent in our portfolios. The stop loss is a good tool most of the time except when there is a flash crash.

    If the criteria have been faithfully followed and it does not work well, check out whether your criteria are wrong, or it does not work on the current market conditions.

3. When we have too many stocks in the same sector, we will want to replace some stocks to better diversify our portfolios.

   When the sector is rising, we want to weigh more on that sector at the expense of diversification, and vice versa. Set a limit of how many sectors you should hold.

4. Need cash for living expenses.

5. To reduce a tax burden by selling some losers. Tax consideration should not be the primary reason for selling. Take advantage of the favorable tax treatment for long-term capital gains. In short, sell losers within the short term limit (currently a year), and sell winners after 365 days; check the current tax laws.

   Harvest tax losses. Sell losers and buy back similar stocks (or same stock after 31 days to avoid wash sale). It is not too clear in which you can buy back the same loser in your children's account under the current tax law.

6. To take advantage of a lower tax. In 2013, we can pay virtually zero (except the increase of tax on social security payment) Federal income taxes on long-term capital gains when our income is below a specific tax bracket (15% as of 2015). Check out the current tax laws. Evaluate the sold winners for a possible buy back.

## Market Timing

7. When the market or the sector plunges, sell stocks or stocks within the sector.

   For temporary peaks, evaluate which stocks in your portfolio to sell based on fundamentals. The objective is to raise cash for buying opportunities.

## Deteriorating appreciation potential

8. There may be some stocks that have a better appreciation potential than the ones you currently own. Churning the portfolio by replacing better stocks may cost some brokerage commissions (some are free

today) and taxes for taxable accounts, but it improves the quality and the appreciation potential for the entire portfolio.

9.  The company's fundamentals have changed for the worse. If you use a scoring system, compare the current score with the score you actually bought the stock for. Apple is a good example from 2013 to 2015. Buy when the fundamentals are good and sell when they are not.

    The basic fundamentals are expected P/E, the quarter-to-quarter earnings growth rate / the sales growth rate, and Debt /Equity.

    When your stocks have passed the peak and started to decline, sell them. When they are heading to bankruptcy, sell them fast.

## Hints that the fundamentals are degrading

Evaluate the stocks you own at least every 6 months and check their daily news at least once a week that can be easily done using Seeking Alpha's portfolio function.

- The cash flow is decreasing fast. Cash flow is not a particularly good predicative indicator for appreciation, but a good indicator on whether the company will survive. This metric is very hard to manipulate.

- A new or pending lawsuit. Check out how serious the lawsuit is and be aware that a minor lawsuit can be ignored. Companies always sue against each other.

- A big drop in sales. Do not be alarmed when a new product, or a new drug is going to replace a major product. Compare sales to the same quarter of prior year to avoid seasonal fluctuations (Q-to-Q info I available from Finviz.com).

- Management deteriorates- One hint is the deteriorating ROE from the last quarter.

- The extravagant life style of the CEO and the many easy loans to officers.

- Poor operations. They include recalls of products such as the GM recall on ignition switches, product secrets being stolen and customers' credit card info being stolen. Boeing's 747-Max is a warning call.

- A successful product from the competitor, or the current product is losing its market share, or becoming a low-profit commodity.

- Insiders and/or institutional investors are dumping the companies' stocks far more than the averages (2% for me) especially in heavy volumes and by more than one insider.

    o Have more than one insider dumping a lot of the stock within a month and no insider purchase in that month.

    o Have more than one insider decrease their holdings by more than 10%.

- When the SEC or any government agency pays attention to a company, it usually means bad news.

- Deceptive accounting practices have been discovered.

- Increasing receivable and/or inventory at an alarming rate.

- Earnings have been restated too many times.

- Short percentage is increasing fast – someone found something wrong with the company.

- The invalidity of 'one-time charges'.

- Abnormal return rate of the company's pension fund comparing to the average of the companies in the same sector.

- Too many and too costly reconstructing charges.

- The entire stock market is plunging as indicated by our chart in detecting market crashes.

- The stock price does not move up with good news. It shows the price has peaked.

- The accumulation amount is far less than the sold amount. When the stock price is up, the accumulation is less than the sold stocks when the stock price was down the last time. It indicates that no more accumulation is ahead and hence the stock will be down most likely.

**Afterthoughts**

- Another article on this topic.
  http://buzz.money.cnn.com/2013/04/05/stocks-sell/
  An article from Investopedia. Nothing new but it is worth having the same second opinion.
  http://www.investopedia.com/financial-edge/0412/5-tips-on-when-to-sell-your-stock.aspx

- It also depends on your strategies. I sell most of my stocks in my momentum portfolio within a month. At least one strategy I know of does not keep any stock during the peak stage of the market cycle – the easiest time to make money but also the riskiest time.

  If you use charts for trading, sell the stocks that are below your moving averages or other technical analysis indicators. Personally I do not use charts for making sell decisions due to my limited time.

- Sell when the company is heading into bankruptcy as described before. The red flags are: 1. Negative cash flow. 2. Heavy insiders dumping the stocks. 3. Pending major lawsuit. 4. Fraud from the management.

- Risky periods for a stock.
  Earnings announcement (4 times a year), settling a major lawsuit and/or during a FDA event in approving a drug are risky periods for a stock. A fluctuation more than 5% in either direction is normal. Some use options to buy insurance. Most ignore it. For the majority of the time, heavy insider purchase is a good indicator. There are rumors (or educated guesses) on earnings before their announcements. Zacks is supposed to be a good subscription for earnings estimates.

# 9     Sectors to be cautious with

There are many reasons to be very cautious when investing in the following sectors. However, Technical Analysis (a.k.a. charting) would give you more hints than the fundamentals for stocks for these sectors. If the big guys are dumping, most likely Technical Analysis (or the simplest SMA-20) would tell you that.

## Loan companies/banks

The financial statements do not show the quality of their loan portfolios. Following this advice, you may be able to skip the banks that melted down in 2007. The peak of Citigroup is $550 and several banks went bankrupt.

Many metrics are not relevant for banks such as Debt/Equity and EBIT. The rising interest rate would be good for banks' profits.

## Drug (generic is ok)

Understanding the complexities of the drug pipelines, its potential profits for new drugs and the expiration of the current drugs may not worth the effort for most retail investors. In addition, a serious lawsuit and / or a serious problem with a drug could wipe out a good percentage of the stock price. When a drug shows unpromising sign(s) in any trial phase, the stock could plunge and vice versa.

## Miners

It is extremely difficult to estimate how much ore (sometimes a miner owns several different types of ores and/or of different grades in the same or different mines) that a company has. It is further complicated by the complexities to extract and transport them. When the total of these costs is greater than its production price, the company will not be profitable. Understanding the market for ore futures is another discipline.

Many mining companies are in foreign countries such as Canada, Australia and countries in South America. Their financial statements of Canada and Australia are more trustworthy than most other emerging countries.

One potential problem of mining companies from many emerging countries is nationalization.

Mining rare earth ore is extremely risky when the profit depends on how China, a major producer of these ores, will price these ores. After China announced the export restrictions on rare earth elements, several non-Chinese companies announced to reopen their mines for rare earths, but few have made any profits as of 2013. Developed countries have stricter environmental regulations.

Coal and eventually oil suffer from the rising use of cleaner energy such as solar and wind.

**Insurance companies**

Insurance companies profit by:

1. The difference between the total premiums received and the total claims minus expenses in running the company.

2. How well they invest the premiums; you pay your premiums earlier than you may collect from any claims.

They can protect the profits in #1 by restricting claims by natural disasters such as earthquakes and by re-insuring. However, a bad disaster could wipe out a lot of their profits.

Even if the insurance company shows you its investment portfolio, most of us, the retail investors, do not have the time and expertise to analyze it.

**Emerging countries (not a sector)**

Their financial statements especially from small companies cannot be trusted, and many countries use different accounting standards. Emerging countries are where the economic growth is. I trade FXI, an ETF, rather than individual Chinese companies. I have lost a lot in small Chinese companies due to frauds and politics. To check out whether the stock is an ADR, try ADR.COM (https://www.adr.com/).

**Stocks with low volumes (not a sector)**

Most likely you pay a high spread to trade these stocks. They can be manipulated easier. I had a hard time trying to sell a stock owned by a few owners.

For simplicity, I trade stocks with the average daily trade volume over 6,000 shares (double it if the price is $2 or less). A better way could be by calculating the percent of your trade quantity / average daily trade volume; it would reduce the effect of penny stocks that have larger volumes due to the low prices.

**Good business and bad business**

Banking is a good business in a growing economy. My deposit in them makes virtually zero interest, and they loan the same money making 3%. If they are more cautious in loaning, they should make good profits.

Restaurant is an easy business to run, but it is very hard to make good money. With the rising of minimal wages, it will get even tougher. That could be the reason for so many coupons today. The high-end restaurants are doing better due to the rising stock market. The pandemic of 2020 would wipe out a lot of small restaurants.

Retailing is a tough business. Look at the top 10 retailers 15 years ago, I can only find two including Macy's that are still surviving. Most are either went bankrupt or being acquired. Even Macy's was not in good financial shape. Amazon is the killer.

Airlines are a tough business. You can tell by the average increase in fares in the last 10 years. It cannot even beat inflation. They have to charge you for everything. The next frontier charge is the rest room (especially for long-distance flights). Now I understand why they call themselves "Frontier Air". As of 2014, it is quite profitable due to mergers and lower fuel cost. The pandemic of 2020 may be the toughest time for airlines. As of 5/2020, Boeing has many serious troubles and they can only survive with a bailout from the government.

There are several software companies that produce software such as the virus detecting programs and tax preparation software. The customers faithfully buy new versions every year. That's great business.

## Appendix 1 – All my books

- Complete the Art of Investing (highly recommended combining most of my books on investing). The Kindle version has over 850 pages (6*9). Investing for lazy investors is a version for beginners.

- Sector Rotation: 21 Strategies and another book Shorting (highly recommended for short-term investors) have more specific chapters on the topic and share many articles with "Complete the art of investing".

- Best stocks as of July, 2021. Not a promise: Another "Best stocks" books available on July 15 and Dec. 15 every year.

- Books for today's market: Profit from Coming Market Crash.
- The following books are in a series: Finding Profitable Stocks, Market Timing and Scoring Stocks. Alternate book Using Fidelity.com.

- Books on strategies: "Profit from bull, bear and sideways markets" (Rotation + Momentum + ETF Rotation + trend following), Trading System (similar to printed version of Complete), Swing (Rotation + Momentum), ETF Rotation for Couch Potatoes, Momentum, SuperStocks, Dividend, Penny & Micro Stock, and Retiree.

- Books for advance beginners: Be an expert (highly recommended), Introduce, Investing for Beginners, Beat Fund Managers, Profit via ETFs, Buffett, Ideas, Conservative, Billionaire and Top-Down.
- Miscellaneous: Lessons in Investing. Investing Strategies. Buy Low and Sell High. Buy High and sell Higher. Buffettology. Technical Analysis. Trading Stocks.
- Concise Editions and Introduction Editions are available at very low prices and are competitive with books of similar sizes (50 pages) and prices ($3 range).

Most books have paperbacks. Links and offers are subject to change without notice.

# Appendix 2 – Complete the Art of Investing

Instead of buying 16 books, why not buy one book (Complete the Art of Investing) consisting of 16 books? Besides saving money and your digital shelve space, it gives you quick reference and concentration on the topic you're currently interested in. It covers most investing topics in investing excluding speculative investing such as currency trading and day trading.

The Kindle version has about 850 pages (6*9), about the size of three books of average size. With the cost of $10 and at least 850 investing ideas, it is about one cent per idea. Most other books have only a few ideas in the entire book

**The 16 books**

This book "Complete Art of Investing" is divided into 16 books as follows. Click for the link to the book described in Amazon.com. I squeezed more than 3,000 pages into 850 pages by eliminating duplicated information such as evaluating stocks.

| Book No. | Amazon.com |
|---|---|
| 1 | Simple techniques |
| 2 | Finding Stocks |
| 3 | Evaluating Stocks |
| 4 | Scoring Stocks |
| 5 | Trading Stocks |
| 6 | Market Timing |
| 7 | Strategies |
| 8 | Sector Rotation |
| 9 | Insider Trading |
| 10 | Penny Stocks & Micro Cap |
| 11 | Momentum Investing |
| 12 | Dividend Investing |
| 13 | Technical Analysis |
| 14 | Investing Ideas |
| 15 | The Economy |
| 16 | Buffettology |

The book links are subject to change without notice.

"How to be a billionaire" is for beginners and couch potatoes, who can use the advanced features of this book in the simplest and less time-consuming techniques. Most advance users can skip this section unless they want to use some of the short cuts described.

We start with the basic books Finding Stocks, Evaluate Stocks, Trading Stocks and Market Timing. You can select and start with one of the many styles and strategies in investing such as swing trading and top-down strategy. Many tools are described in other books such as ETFs, technical analysis, covered calls and trading plan.

Many books start with "Why" to lure you to read more and are followed by "How" and then the theory behind the book.
If the book you're reading is beneficial to you, imagine how it would with 850 pages.

---

\#

Most readers' comments are on "Debunk the Myths in Investing", which this book is originally based on. As of 2018, I did not know any of the commentators on my books.

"I skipped ahead to his chapter book 14 (of "Complete the Art of Investing"), Investment Advice just to get a feel of his writing style. His research is phenomenal and doesn't overwhelm with big words or catchy "sales-like" tactics.

I truly believe this ordinary man, Mr. Tony Pow, has a gift of explaining his experience as an investor without the bull crap of trying to make you buy his stuff. He seemingly just wants to share his knowledge, tips, and clarity of definitions for the kind of folks like me who want to understand something FIRST before jumping in with emotions of trying to make a boat load of money. I like the technical analysis side he brings.

Mr. Tony Pow talks about hidden gems in his book; well....quite frankly, he is a hidden gem. Thank you and I will also post my comments about this author to my Facebook page!" – JB on this book.

"Excellent book, recommend to all investors... great knowledge. It has fine-tuned my investing strategies... Your book is hard to set aside, as I read it all the time learning good techniques and analysis of stocks, ETF... Since I purchased your book in March, I have underlined, highlighted and placed tabs on top of pages for quick reference." – Aileron on this book.

"Tony, I just finished reading your 2nd edition. It's my pleasure to report that I found it most interesting. You're welcome to use this blurb if you like:

Debunk the Myths in Investing is an all-encompassing look at not only the most salient factors influencing markets and investors, but also a from-the-trenches look at many of the misconceptions and mistakes too many investors make. Reading this book may save not only time and aggravation but money as well!"

Joseph Shaefer, CEO, Stanford Wealth Management LLC.

"Tony, Great work!" from James and Chris, who are portfolio managers.

"'Debunk the Myths in Investing' is a comprehensive book on investing that deals with many aspects of this tense profession in which with a lot of knowledge and a bit of luck (or vice versa) one can greatly benefit...

Therefore 'Debunk the Myths in Investing' is an interesting book that on its 500 pages offer a lot of knowledge related to investing world and many practical advice, so I can recommend its reading if you're interested in this topic."
- Denis Vukosav, Top 500 Reviewers at Amazon.com.

"490 pages (Debunk) of a genius's ranting and hypothesis with various theories throughout, written light-heartedly with ample doses of humor...Yes, the myth of not being able to profitably time the market is BUSTED...

One might ask... Why is he giving away the results of his hard-earned research for only $20? He states that his children are not interested in investing and wants to share his efforts with the world." - Abe Agoda.

"Excellent book, recommend to all investors... great knowledge. It has fine-tuned my investing strategies... Your book is hard to set aside, as I read it all the time learning good techniques and analysis of stocks, ETF... Since I purchased your book in March, I have underlined, highlighted and placed tabs on top of pages for quick reference." - Aileron on this book.

"Great stuff, Tony. It's great to meet experienced traders such as yourself. I had a browse through the book and think your method is a little more refined than mine."

"Your strategy is very rules based and solid. I sometimes envy people who have developed something like this."

## Making 50% in one month

I claim to have the best one-month performance ever for recommending 8 or more stocks without using options and leverage. My following return is 57% in a month or 621% annualized. They are slightly different as I calculated the average from the averages of three different accounts. The average buy date is 12/26/18 and the "current date" is 01/28/19.

The performance may not be repeated. I will use the same screen for the coming years and even the expected 10% (or 120% annualized) is very good.

I used the same screen for searching stock candidates. I spent a total of about 20 hours from Dec. 15, 2018 to Jan. 5, 2019.

| Stock | Buy Price | Sold or Current Price | Buy date | Sold or Current date | Profit % | Profit % Ann. | Status |
|---|---|---|---|---|---|---|---|
| CHK | 2.13 | 2.99 | 01/03/09 | 01/18/19 | 40% | 982% | Sold |
| MNK | 16.41 | 21.45 | 01/03/19 | 01/25/19 | 31% | 510% | Sold |
| MNK | 16.43 | 21.45 | 01/03/19 | 01/25/19 | 31% | 507% | Sold |
| NNBR | 5.68 | 8.58 | 12/26/18 | 01/28/19 | 51% | 565% | |
| NNBR | 5.72 | 8.58 | 12/26/18 | 01/28/19 | 66% | 727% | |
| ESTE | 4.35 | 6.45 | 12/26/18 | 01/18/19 | 48% | 766% | Sold |
| LCI | 4.61 | 8.29 | 12/21/18 | 01/28/19 | 80% | 767% | |
| MDR | 8.01 | 9.13 | 01/08/19 | 01/28/19 | 14% | 255% | |
| YRCW | 3.29 | 5.78 | 12/21/18 | 01/28/19 | 76% | 727% | |
| YRCW | 3.26 | 5.78 | 12/21/18 | 01/28/19 | 77% | 742% | |
| ASRT | 3.56 | 4.18 | 12/26/18 | 01/28/19 | 17% | 193% | |
| UTCC | 7.13 | 11.00 | 12/26/18 | 01/28/19 | 54% | 600% | |
| YRCW | 2.92 | 5.78 | 12/26/18 | 01/28/19 | 98% | 1083% | |

## Best one-year return

I claim to have the best-performed article in Seeking Alpha history, an investing site, for recommending 15 or more stocks in one year after the publish date without using options and leverage.

https://seekingalpha.com/article/1095671-amazing-returns-velti-alcatel-lucent-alpha-natural-resources

## Your choice

"Complete the art of investing" should be your first choice. If you are short-term trading, I recommend "Sector Rotation: 21 Strategies" and "Shorting Stocks /ETFs". These 3 books together with "Using Fidelity" share many articles.

My recommended stocks can be found in my "Best stocks" series. It would be published in July 1 and in Dec. 15 – it is not a promise. So far, this book and "Sector Rotation: 21 Strategies" are my best sellers. All info are subject to change without notice.

## Sector Rotation: 21 Strategies

In addition, as of 5/2020 I bet that no author besides me made **over 4 times** using sector rotation starting the amount more than his yearly salary then.

- On 5/26/2020, I searched for "Sector Rotation" under Amazon's Book. They are listed in the same order except my book Sector Rotation: 21 Strategies.

| Book | Date | Size[1] | Kindle $[1] | Hard $ |
|---|---|---|---|---|
| Sector Rotation: 21 Strategies | **05/2020** | **425** | **$9.95** | $24.95 |
| Super Sectors | 09/2010 | 289 | $26.39 | $49.95 |
| Dual Momentum Investing | 11/2014 | 240 | $40.40 | $42.20 |
| Sector Investing | 05/1996 | 260 | | $29.94 |
| Sector Trading Strategies | 08/2007 | 164 | $26.39 | $16.66 |
| The Sector Strategist | 03/2012 | 225 | $26.39 | $44.96 |
| ETF Rotation | 10/2012 | 125 | **$9.95** | **$14.99** |
| Optimal... Sector Rotation | 07/2015 | 80 | | $44.07 |

[1] From Amazon on size and prices as of 5/25/2020. Last update is 09/2021.

My book won in all categories except the price for hard copy in one. However, my book won as the lowest cost per page by a wide margin.

- I have **21** strategies in sector rotation while most books have only one. It ranges from simple rotation of a stock ETF and cash for beginners to many advanced strategies for experts. Most other books have one or two strategies.
- Andrew, a contributor on Sector Rotation article at Seeking Alpha, said, "Great stuff, Tony. It's great to meet experienced traders such as yourself. I had a browse through the book and think your method is a little more refined than mine."

- "You have written the book in a way that makes good and logical sense." Bill.
- Do not be fooled by past performances. Just check the recent performance of the top 50 stocks selected by IBD in the last five years. The mediocre result (hopefully it will change) could be due to too many followers and/or there is no evergreen strategy.
- I switched most (if not all) of my sector funds in April, 2000 from technology sectors to traditional sectors (better to money market fund). We can reduce losses by spotting market plunges and the sector trend.

## Best stocks to buy as of July, 2021

We care about performance only. Not considering dividends and fees, my last three books in this series have beaten the SPY (the market to most) by **110%, 71% and 25%** from the publish date to 07/01/2021.

My new book in this series titled "Best stocks to buy as of July, 2021" has been just released in Amazon.com on 07/15/2021. For more description, please click here, or type the following in your browser: https://www.amazon.com/dp/B099KQ9DSV

| Book | Stocks | Return | Ann. | Beat SPY by |
|------|--------|--------|------|-------------|
| Best Book for 2021 2nd Edition | 10 | 20% | 52% | 110% |
| Best Book for 2021 | 4 | 29% | 52% | 71% |
| Best Book to Buy from Aug, 2020 | 14 | 42% | 45% | 25% |
| Avg. | 9 | 31% | 50% | 69% |

The following are not promises. I plan to release a new book in this series titled "Best Stocks" on 12/15 each year. I may release my techniques for retail investors and institution investors for one-time charges. Contact me at pow_tony@yahoo.com if you are interested.

## Appendix 3 - Our window to the investing world

The paperback version of this chapter can be found in the following link. http://ebmyth.blogspot.com/2013/11/web-sites.html

- **General**

Wikipedia / Investopedia /Yahoo!Finance / MarketWatch / Cnnfn / Morningstar /CNBC / Bloomberg / WSJ / Barron's / Motley Fool / TheStreet

- **Evaluate stocks**
  Finviz / SeekingAlpha / MSN Money / Zacks / Daily Finance / ADR / Fidelity / BlueChipGrowth / Earnings Impact / OpenInsider / NYSE / NASDAQ / SEC / SEC for 10K and 10Q (quarterly) reports required to file for listed stocks in major exchanges.
- **Charts**
  BigCharts / FreeStockCharts / StockCharts /
- **Screens**
  Yahoo!Finance / Finviz / CNBC / Morningstar /
- **Besides stocks**
  123Jump / Hoover's Online / FINRA Bond Market Data / REIT / Commodity Futures / Option Industry
- **Vendors**
  AAII / Zacks / IBD / GuruFocus / VectorVest / Fidelity / Interactive Brokers / Merrill Lynch /
- **Economy.**
  Econday / EcoconStats / Federal Reserve / Economist /
- **Misc.**
  Dow Jones Indices / Russell / Wilshire / IRS / Wikinvest / ETF Database / ETF Trends / Nolo (estate planning) / AARP /

## Appendix 4 - ETFs / Mutual Funds

**What is an ETF**

ETFs have basic differences from mutual funds: 1. Lower management expenses, 2. Trade ETFs same as stocks, and 3. Usually more diversified but not more selective than the related mutual funds such as NOBL vs FRDPX.

The major classifications of ETFs are 1. Simulating an index such as SPY, QQQ and DIA, 2. Simulating a sector such as XLE and SOXX, 3. Simulating an asset class such as GLD and SLV, 4. Simulating a country or a group of countries such as EWC and FXI, 5. Managed by a manager(s) such as ARKK, 6. Betting a market or sector to go down such as SH and PSQ, and 7. Leveraged (not recommended for beginners).

Fidelity: Index ETFs (https://www.fidelity.com/etfs/overview).

Wikipedia on ETF (http://en.wikipedia.org/wiki/Exchange-traded_fund).

**List of ETFs**
ETF data base (Recommended): http://etfdb.com/
ETF Bloomberg: http://www.bloomberg.com/markets/etfs/
ETF Trends: http://www.etftrends.com/
A list of ETFs. Seeking Alpha.
http://etf.stock-encyclopedia.com/category/)
A list of contra ETFs (or bear ETFs)
http://www.tradermike.net/inverse-short-etfs-bearish-etf-funds/
Misc.: ETFGuide, ETFReplay
Fidelity low-cost index funds:
https://www.youtube.com/watch?v=zpKi4_IJvlY
Fidelity Annuity funds with performance data.
http://fundresearch.fidelity.com/annuities/category-performance-annual-total-returns-quarterly/FPRAI?refann=005

**Other resources**
Most subscription services offer research on ETFs. IBD has a strategy dedicated to ETFs and so does AAII to name a couple.

Seeking Alpha has extensive resources for ETF including an ETF screener and investing ideas. So is ETFdb.

**Not all ETFs are created equal**
Check their performances and their expenses.

**When to use or not to use ETFs**
I prefer sector mutual funds in some industries, as they have many bad stocks such as drug industry, banks, miners and insurers. Most mutual funds cannot time the market.

When you believe a sector is heading up (or contra ETF for heading down), but you do not have time to do research on specific stocks, buy an ETF for the sector; it is same for the market.

**Half ETF**
Taking out half of the stocks that score below the average in an index ETF could beat the same full ETF itself. I call it HETF (half the ETF). You heard it here first. To illustrate, sort the expected P/E (not including stocks with negative earnings) in ascending order and only include the stocks on the first half. Add more fundamental metrics. It will take a few minutes.

**Disadvantages of ETFs**
- When you have two stocks in a sector ETF one good one and one bad one, the ETF treats them the same. Stock pickers would buy the one that has a better appreciation potential.
- Sometimes the return could be misleading due to stock rotation. To illustrate this, on August 29, 2012, SHLD was replaced by LYB in a sector fund. SHLD was down by 4% and LYB was up by 4% primarily due to the switch. Unless you sell and buy at the right time (which is impossible), your return would not match the ETF's returns due to the replacement.
- Ensure the performance matches the corresponding index; it is hard due to excluding dividends.

**Advantages of ETFs**
- We have demonstrated that you can beat the market by using market timing. Between 2000 and Nov., 2013, you only exit and reenter the market 3 times and the result is astonishing.
- It is easy to rotate a sector vs. buying/selling all of the stocks in this sector. Rotating a sector is the same as trading a stock.
- The risk is spread out, and your portfolio is diversified especially for a market ETF or buying three or more ETFs in different sectors.
- Periodically the bad stocks in most funds are replaced by better stocks.
- Eliminate the time in researching stocks.

**Leveraged ETFs**
I do not recommend them. Some are 2x, 3x and even higher. They're too risky for beginners. However, when you are very sure or your tested strategy has very low drawdown, you may want to use them to improve performance. Most leveraged ETFs and contra ETFs have higher fees.

**My basic ETF tables**
I include some contra ETFs, mutual funds and Fidelity's annuity. Some of these may be interesting to you.

ETFs and funds come and go. Some ideas and classifications are my own interpretation. Refer to ETFdb for updated information. Not responsible for any error. Check out the ETF or fund before you take any action.

Table by market cap:

| Category | ETF | Mutual Funds | Fidelity's Annuity | Contra ETF | Alternate |
|---|---|---|---|---|---|
| Size: | | | | | |
| Large Cap | DIA | See Blend | | DOG | |
| | SPY | | | SH | FXAIX VOO |
| | QQQ | | | PSQ | FNCMX |
| | RYH | | | | |
| Blend | IWD | BEQGX | | | |
| Growth | SPYG | FBGRX | | | FSPGX |
| Value | SPYV | DOGGX | | | FLCOX |
| Dividend | NOBL | FRDPX | | | |
| | VYM | | | | |
| | | | | | |
| Mid Cap | | | FNBSC | MYY | |
| Blend | MDY | VSEQX | | | |
| Growth | | STDIX | | | |
| | | BPTRX | | | |
| Value | | FSMVX | | | |
| | | | | | |
| Small Cap | | | FPRGC | SBB | FSSNX |
| Blend | IWM | HDPSX | | | |
| Growth | | PRDSX | | | FECGX |
| Value | | SKSEX | | | FISVX |
| | | | | | |
| Micro | IWC | | | | |
| | | | | | |
| Multi | | | | | |

| | | | | | |
|---|---|---|---|---|---|
| Blend | | VDEOX | | | |
| Growth | | VHCOX | | | |
| Value | | TCLCX | | | |
| Total | | | | | FSKAX |
| Bond | | | | | |
| Long Term (20) | VLV | BTTTX | | TBF | |
| Mid Term (7 – 10) | VCIT | FSTGX | | | |
| Short Term (1 – 3 yrs.) | VCSH | THOPX | | | |
| Total | BOND | PONDX | | | |
| Corp Invest Grade | VCIT | NTHEX | | | |
| High Yield (junk) | PHB | SPHIX | | | |
| Muni | MUB | Check state | | | |
| | | | | | |
| Special situation | | | | | |
| Buy back | PKW | | | | |
| | | | | | |

Table by sectors:

| Sector | ETF | Mutual Funds | Fidelity's Annuity |
|---|---|---|---|
| Banking[1] | | FSRBK | |
| Regional | IAT | | |
| Bio Tech | IBB | FBIOX | |
| | XBI | Large | |
| Consumer Dis. | XLY | FSCPX | FVHAC |
| Consumer Staple | XLP | FDFAX | FCSAC |
| | | | |
| Finance | KIE | FIDSX | FONNC |
| | IYF | | |
| Energy | XLE | FSENX | FJLLC |
| Energy Service | | FSESX | |
| Gold | GLD | FSAGX | |
| Gold Miner | GDX | VGPMX | |
| Health Care | IYH | FSPHX | FPDRC |
| | VHT | VGHCX | |
| House Builder | ITB | FSHOX | |
| | ITB | Perform | |

| Industrial | IYJ | FCYIX | FBALC |
|---|---|---|---|
| | | | |
| Material | VAW | FSDPX | |
| | IYM | | |
| | | | |
| Oil | USO | | |
| Oil Service | OIH | FSESX | |
| Oil Exploration | XOP | | |
| Real Estate | VNQ | FRIFX | FFWLC |
| REIT | VNQ | | |
| | | | |
| Retail | RTH | FSRPX | |
| | XRT | | |
| Regional bank | KRE | FSRBX | |
| | | | |
| Semi Conduct | SMH | | |
| Software | XSW | FSCSX | |
| | IGV | | |
| Technology | XLK | FSPTX | FYENC |
| | FDN | FBSOX | |
| | | ROGSX | |
| | | | |
| Telecomm. | VOX | FSTCX | FVTAC |
| Transport | XTN | | |
| | IYT | | |
| Utilities | XLU | FSUTX | FKMSC |
| | | | |
| Wireless | | FWRLX | |

Footnote. [1] Also check Finance.

Table by countries outside the USA:

| Country | ETF | Mutual Funds | Fidelity's Annuity | Alternate |
|---|---|---|---|---|
| Australia | EWA | | | |
| Brazil | EWZ | | | |
| Canada | EWC | FICDX | | |
| China | FXI | FHKCX | | |
| EAFE | EFA | | | |
| Emerging | VWO | FEMEX | FEMAC | FPADX |
| Europe | VGK | FIEUX | | |
| Global | KXI | PGVFX | | |
| Greece | GREK | | | |
| India | INDY | MINDX | | |
| Indonesia | EIDO | | | |
| Latin America | ILF | FLATX | | |
| Nordic | | FNORX | | |
| | | | | |
| Hong Kong | EWH | | | |
| Japan | EWJ | FJPNX | | |
| S. Africa | EZA | | | |
| S. Korea | EWY | MAKOX | | |
| Singapore | EWS | | | |
| Taiwan | EWT | | | |
| | TUR | | | |
| United Kingdom | EWU | | | |
| Foreign: | | | | |
| Combination | | | | |
| Intern. Div. | IDV | | | FTIHX |
| Small Cap | SCZ | | | |
| Value | EFV | | | |
| Europe | VGK | | | |
| | | | | |

#Filler: Honey, my book can play music.
https://www.youtube.com/watch?v=HxGT5z6d-GA&list=PLMZa6mP7jZ2b1otqG4tfbgZpLEdh6YiNF

It may cut down commercials by casting it to TV.

www.ingramcontent.com/pod-product-compliance
Lightning Source LLC
Chambersburg PA
CBHW071752170526
45167CB00003B/1000